Grapevine St

Stick Figuring through the Bible

Old Testament Overview

A Chronological Study of the Major Characters and Events
of the Old Testament

Teacher Edition   Level 3-4

Grapevine Studies
P.O. Box 2123
Glenrock, WY 82637
(877) 436-2317

Web site: www.grapevinestudies.com

Email: info@grapevinestudies.com

Old Testament Overview
Level 3-4
Teacher Edition

By Dianna Wiebe

©2005 by Grapevine Studies

ISBN 1-59873-017-7

Maps are courtesy of Steven Gordon of Cartagram LLC, www.cartagram.com

Cover design by Sean Athey of Profession Print Management, www.proprintman.com.

Old Testament Overview

Level 3-4

Dedication

This lesson series is dedicated to my children Cody, Tabitha, Luke, and Zak. Isaiah 59:21

I would also like to dedicate this book to all those parents and teachers who desire to diligently teach their children and their students the Word of God.

Acknowledgments

I would first like to thank the Lord God Almighty for His faithfulness to me through the years to me. The inspiration, the creativity, and the ideas for this study have all come from Him.

I would like to thank my beloved husband, John, for his spiritual leadership and oversight of this large project, for his prayers, advice, encouragement, and support! If he hadn't laughed and loved my first stick-figured lessons, I never would have attempted this book!

Thank you Dave and Janet Bowman, for boldly teaching what no one had taught before! Thank you for piloting this program with me--you have given me great advice and been a great encouragement!

Thank you Brian and Kim Peil for your constant encouragement--you've taught me what determination means.

A special thank you goes to Mary Jo Tate for editing our books--it has been a pleasure to work with you on this project.

The Inspiration

Deuteronomy 6:4-7

Hear, O Israel: The Lord our God, the Lord is one! You shall love the Lord your God with all your heart, with all your soul, and with all your strength. And these words which I command you today shall be in your heart. You shall teach them diligently to your children, and shall talk of them when you sit in your house, when you walk by the way, when you lie down, and when you rise up.

Psalm 78:4b-7

...Telling to the generation to come the praises of the Lord, and His strength and His wonderful works that He has done. For He established a testimony in Jacob, and appointed a law in Israel, which He commanded our fathers, that they should make them known to their children; that the generation to come might know them, the children who would be born, that they may arise and declare them to their children, that they may set their hope in God, and not forget the works of God, but keep His commandments.

Table of Contents

The Grapevine Mission

Our mission at Grapevine Studies is to provide believers with a method and curriculums to study the Bible, using a timeline, stick figures, words, symbols, and colors to teach chronological lessons.

The Grapevine Method

Grapevine Studies teaches the Bible as if it were a puzzle, doing the frame first. Once the framework is in place (the timeline) then individual pieces (Bible passages, characters, and events) are much easier to place and understand in the context of the "whole puzzle" (the whole counsel of the Word of God).

This lesson series will first introduce and teach the Old Testament timeline. Each subsequent lesson will begin with a **timeline review** up to the point of that day's lesson. As students **read** the Bible lessons they will be able to place their "puzzle pieces" into their framework (timeline) and have an understanding of the context of the character/event they are reading about. Students read passages from the Bible and **draw** (or take notes on) each section of Scripture, using what we at Grapevine Studies call **stick figuring**. Stick figuring is using stick figures, symbols, colors, charts, and words to illustrate each Bible passage. This method allows students to interact with the Bible passage and be as creative as they desire. At the end of each lesson a set of **review questions** is given to ensure that students have grasped the essentials of the passage (the who, what, where, when, why, and how). **Application** of the lesson is for the teacher to determine based upon prayer, the class, the needs of individual students, and what that teacher feels the Lord has led him to emphasize. Each lesson ends with a Bible **memory verse** that is related to the lesson and the timeline.

The *Old Testament Overview* ends with a review of the series' timeline and memory verses. By the end of this series your student should be able to complete the entire Old Testament timeline alone. In addition, students should know several facts regarding each character and event they have studied and know where the books of the Bible fit into the timeline. Students will also be very familiar with using Bible study tools including, a topical Bible, Bible concordance, and Bible dictionary.

Our prayer is that those who take this journey, both teachers and students, will expand in their knowledge of the Bible and grow in their love for the Lord and His Word. May God bless you richly as you study and teach His Word!

The Grapevine Studies Statement of Faith

Bible: We believe that the Bible is the inspired, infallible, authoritative, complete Word of God and is accurate in all historical and scientific references.

God: We believe that there is one holy and perfect God, externally existent in three persons—Father, Son, and Holy Spirit.

Jesus: We believe that Jesus Christ is true God and true man; in His virgin birth, sinless life, miracles, atoning death, bodily resurrection, ascension, and in His physical return.

Holy Spirit: We believe that the Holy Spirit is the divine third person of the triune God, sent to indwell, comfort, teach, empower the believer; and to convict the unbeliever of sin.

Man: We believe man was originally created perfect, in the image and likeness of God, with an unbroken relationship to God. When the first man (Adam) disobeyed God, the perfect relationship that God and man was broken and the curse of sin and death entered all creation. All men are born with this sin nature and only the atoning work of the Lord Jesus Christ can remove man's sinful nature and restore the broken relationship with God.

Salvation: We believe that salvation (forgiveness of sin against God) is provided only through faith in the life, death, resurrection, and ascension of Jesus Christ for all me who believe, repent, and receive the gift of eternal life. As a result of faith, works will follow.

Resurrection: We believe in the resurrection of both the believer (saved) and the unbeliever (unsaved); the believer to eternal life and the unbeliever to eternal damnation.

Teacher-Directed Doctrine

Grapevine Studies is please to be able to provide Bible curriculum to a variety of denominations. Our unique teacher-directed doctrinal approach provides a platform for each teacher/parent to explain their specific doctrines as they come up with in each lesson.

Grapevine Teacher Goals

Grapevine Studies assumes that teachers of this curriculum will already have a personal and intimate relationship with the Lord, and a calling to teach the Word of God. At Grapevine Studies our goals for teachers are that you will:

- Learn more of the character of the God you serve and His word.
- Be godly examples to your students.
- Effectively communicate the Word of God to this generation of believers.
- Instruct only after having spent time in prayer, Bible reading, and study.
- Have sufficient preparation time for your own study without the need to gather, order, and put together multiple supplies for various activities.
- Learn along with your students.

Grapevine Student Goals

Grapevine Studies believes that students who are taught using reading, hearing, and drawing will have a higher retention rate then those who are just lectured. We also believe that teaching the Bible in a chronological and sequential format is the best for long-term memory and life impact At Grapevine Studies our goals for students are that they will:

- Be introduced to the One that all history pointed toward—Jesus, the Messiah, The Christ. Once students become believers, to teach them to know God and live a holy life.

- See God's interaction and movement through history as He dealt with nations and individuals so that they will be able to recognize God's interaction and movement in their own lives.

- Have a framework of the Bible that will encourage and inspire them to study further on their own, to fill in their own Biblical puzzle, and to understand the context of the passages they read in the future.

- Practice using various Bible study tools: topical Bible, concordance, and Bible dictionary.

- Learn from those who have lived before us.

Teacher and Student Supply List

- Teacher supplies: a Bible, Grapevine Studies Teacher Guide, a dry erase board, dry erase markers of various colors, wall maps, a topical Bible, concordance, and a Bible dictionary.

- Student supplies: a Bible, Grapevine Studies Student Book, pencil or pen, colored pencils, a topical Bible, concordance, and a Bible dictionary.

Teaching Grapevine Lessons

Before Class

Prayer: Nothing can replace the time a teacher spends with our Master Teacher, the Lord God Almighty.

Section Goals and Key Points: As you prepare for your lesson, I recommend a review of the lesson goals and key points at the beginning of each section. These pages are designed to give you a concise summary of the lesson you will be teaching.

Research Links: We have provided research links on our website to aid you in your study. Our website is www.grapevinestudies.com/Links.htm.

Schedule

Weekly (Bible Study or Sunday School Class)

We recommend one lesson each week. Class time can be used to review answers to questions on the Review Page, give presentations of the Activities and Further Study assignments. For a year long study, the fifty lessons included in your book will allow two extra weeks to complete any assignments or to have free for holidays or special events. See Addendum for Weekly Schedule.

Daily (School)

We recommend one page of each lesson, per day, for 175 days to complete a school year. See Addendum for Daily Schedule.

> Day 1: Timeline and memory verse review page.
>
> Day 2: Complete page one of the lesson.
>
> Day 3: Complete page two of the lesson.
>
> Day 4: Level 3 students create the character and event card and review their memory verse for that lesson.

The Timeline

Lesson 1 of this series is an overview of the Old Testament timeline. I have written the teacher notes in such a way that you could read them to your students and then draw each character or event on the board. I recommend that you read over it and become familiar enough with it that you can tell the story in your own words. Remember that this is not a detailed lesson but an overview of the coming year. Throughout the year we will examine each character and event in more detail.

Review Page

The goal of this page is to review the timeline and the memory verses from the past three lessons.

Timeline Review: Level 4 students will draw in the pictures on the timeline and fill in the missing titles below the timeline. Teacher's editions have the pictures drawn in and the missing titles.

Memory Verses: Students will review the previous three memory verses by either writing out the entire verse or filling in the missing words. Memory verse sheets for several Bible versions are available to download from our website www.grapevinestudies.com/Links.htm.

Lesson Pages

Background Bible Reading: This is required reading for teachers. Some lessons encompass a great deal of information that cannot be covered in a single lesson. Teachers will need to determine what information they might want to "fill in" to make the lesson as understandable as possible for their students.

Time Frame: The time frame gives students the context of the lesson.

Section Titles: These titles correspond with the student lessons.

Teacher Notes: The teacher notes, in italic print, explain the important information that will need to be covered in that section of the lesson. These notes will also be helpful for substitute teachers and can even be read to the students if needed. Space has been provided in each section for you to write in your own notes.

Student Pages: Student page (SP) numbers are found in the box at the lower right hand corner of corresponding pages.

Level 3 and Level 4: This combined teacher manual will enable you to teach both levels from one book. Notes, drawings, review questions and answers are the same for both levels.

Look-up Words: This symbol indicates the words that I recommend you look up. This may mean simply looking up the word in a Bible dictionary or *Strong's Concordance*, but it may also mean doing some further research so that you know the function of that word. For example, the word for "priest", your students will need more than just a definition. For priest, you will want them to know where the priest served, the duties a priest performed, why the priests were important, etc. This will allow your students to better understand the context of the passage you are studying, while enabling you to answer questions that might arise regarding these words. All look-up words are from the New King James Version of the Bible, if you are using a different version of the Bible your look-up words may vary slightly.

Maps (Level 3): This symbol indicates that there is a map exercise that goes with that section of the lesson. The parentheses indicate which map to use for that lesson. Map exercises are designed to help students become familiar with the land of the Bible. I recommend comparing various maps and having wall maps to help aid students in understanding locations of cities, countries, and geographical points.

Draw: This is to give you a written description of what I have drawn on lesson pages of the teacher notes. Color choices are up to the teacher and student. We suggest that you use only the color purple to represent God, Jesus Christ, and the Holy Spirit.

Review Questions and Answers: This section gives you the questions and answers for the lesson review. Answers may vary. Please note that the last question of each lesson is "What do we learn about God from these verses?" This is the application question of the lesson. The answer to this question will depend upon what the Lord has led you to emphasize. My answers reflect the way in which I have taught that lesson, but may not be how the Lord will lead you to teach the lesson.

Teaching the Lessons

Reading: Following the short review which will set the time frame for the lesson, the first set of Scriptures will be read (see first Scripture box). If you are teaching Level 3 and Level 4 students at the same time we recommend using the Level 4 scripture readings. If you are teaching only Level 3 students, we recommend using the student edition as a guide for scripture readings.

Drawing: After the Scripture is read, the teacher will then stick figure that portion of Scripture onto the board. Students can either draw what the teacher has drawn or their own interpretation of the Scripture section. I encourage colors and creativity. Some students may opt to take notes in this section.

Lesson Review: At the end of the lesson there will be a lesson review. These questions will cover the who, what, when, where, why, and how of the lesson. Teachers are encouraged to ask additional questions as needed for comprehension and review.

Memory Verse: A memory verse is given at the end of each lesson that will relate to the lesson and the timeline.

Character and Event Cards (Level 3)

Character and Event Cards: On Day 4 of each lesson student will make their Character and Event Cards and review their memory verse. These cards are designed to be memory aids and used for reviews. On the front of each card students will write the title of that card, i.e. Creation. On the back of each card you will have your students put the information you want them to remember about each character or event. If you are teaching multiple levels this assignment is the same for Levels 1 and 2.

Reviews

The goal of the reviews is to show the students what they **have learned**. There are five types of reviews built into this curriculum:

1. Timeline Review: the timeline or a section of the timeline is reviewed at the beginning of each lesson.

2. Lesson Review: at the end of each class.

3. Section Reviews: after each section, every five to six lessons. Each section ends with a review that covers a sampling of the lesson review questions and all the memory verses from that section. There are many ways to do this review without writing out the answer to each question. Be creative!

   - Trivia: Divide the class into two groups or challenge another class to a trivia game using the review questions.

   - Matching: Put the questions and answers on individual pieces of paper and then match them.

   - Teens/Adults Challenge (good for groups or individuals): Each team member is given a list of the Scriptures that were covered in the previous section. Each team takes turns quizzing one another on the facts related to the previous lessons (we use who, what, when, where, why, and how to begin each question). Each team member is allowed to use one index card to write down facts, which must be completed before class. Points are given if the student can answer the question using only his memory and his card (we give 5 points). Fewer points are given if the student has to open his notebook or Bible (we give 2.5 points). A time limit of one minute per question is enforced.

4. Mid-Series Review: at the mid-point of the series. This review covers the timeline and the memory verses to date.

5. Final Review: at the end of the series. The final review covers the Old Testament timeline and all the memory verses from this series. The final review is designed to show students how much of the Old Testament they have learned.

The
Old Testament
Timeline

Section 1 Goals and Key Points

OLD TESTAMENT TIMELINE NARRATIVE

The goal of this lesson is to give the students the outline for the entire lesson series. You will draw the timeline on the board while the students draw it on their notebook sheets. The following key points are a brief explanation of the facts you will want to communicate to your students. As a teacher you will want to become familiar with the key points of the timeline so that you are teaching the timeline in your own words.

Key points:

God In the beginning—God. God was before creation.

Creation In the beginning God created all things in six days and on the seventh day God rested from His work.

Adam and Eve The first man and woman that God created were Adam and Eve. In the beginning Adam and Eve had a complete and unbroken relationship with God (the purple triangle connected to the red heart).

The Fall The Fall of man came when Adam and Eve listened to the serpent and ate the fruit from the tree of the knowledge of good and evil, which God had commanded them not to eat. By eating this fruit, Adam and Eve disobeyed God or sinned against God. Sin caused the relationship between God and Adam and Eve to be broken (purple triangle with broken line to red heart). Sin brought death into the world (insert the words "death" and "sin"). In Genesis we learn that God punished Adam and Eve for their sins. But God also promised that one day a "seed" (man) would be born of a woman and that this man would restore the relationship between God and man. (Add eyes looking right at the top of each page of the Old Testament timeline. From this point on all history looks forward to the "Seed," the Messiah, the Christ). Before Adam and Eve left the Garden of Eden, God provided animal skin coats to clothe them.

Noah Ten generations after Adam, Noah was born. God gave Noah a specific assignment, to build an ark. God was going to flood the earth and the ark would carry Noah, his family, two of each kind of unclean animal, and seven of each kind of clean animal (to be used later for sacrifices and food) so that they would not be killed in the Flood.

The Flood Once Noah had built the ark, God sent the Flood. The fountains in the deep burst open, and the sky opened its floodgates, and it rained forty days and forty nights. Every man and animal not in the ark died in the Flood. After the Flood, God gave man and the animals a promise that He would never again Flood the entire earth. The sign of God's promise was a rainbow.

The Tower After the flood, God commanded man to scatter and fill the earth. Instead men gathered and built a city (Babel) and a tower, which was in direct disobedience to God's command (draw the circle representing the people gathering). As a result, God confused the language of the people, which caused them to scatter over all the earth, creating many different people groups. (Draw four lines coming from the circle, with circles at the end of each line representing the people scattering and forming many people groups).

Job The book of Job records for us the sufferings of Job and his response to his sufferings, as well as God's response to Job's questions.

Abraham Ten generations after Noah God chose to make a very important covenant with a man named Abraham. **The promise** (draw the Star of David) that God made to Abraham was that He would give him a **great name**, make his family into a **great nation**, give him a **specific land**, and that through his family **seed** all the families of the earth would be blessed. God also promised Abraham and his wife, Sarah, that they would have a son, Isaac, through whom the man (seed of woman) would be born. Our second indication of who Messiah would be is found in the promise that God made to Abraham: the Christ would be (1) born of woman and (2) born of the line of Abraham.

Isaac Isaac was born when Abraham was one hundred years old and Sarah was ninety. God made the same covenant with Isaac that He had made with Abraham.

Jacob Jacob was the son of Isaac through whom God continued His covenant. God changed Jacob's name to Israel.

Jacob's children Jacob had twelve sons and one daughter.

Joseph One of Jacob's sons, Joseph, was sold as a slave into Egypt. While in Egypt, Joseph was promoted from a slave to second in command of all Egypt. God used Joseph to prepare Egypt for a famine and to provide food for the people of the region, including his own family.

Egypt Because of the famine, the rest of Jacob/Israel's family moved to Egypt, where they lived for 430 years.

The Bondage Several years after moving to Egypt, the children of Israel went into bondage. For 400 years they labored under hard bondage. While in bondage, the children of Israel cried out to God for a deliverer.

Moses During Israel's bondage, Pharaoh, king of Egypt, became afraid of the numerous children of Israel and ordered all the Hebrew baby boys killed. It is at this time that Moses was born, to a Levite couple. To protect Moses from certain death, his mother placed him in a basket in the Nile River, where he was found and adopted by the Princess of Egypt. Moses grew up in Egypt and at age forty killed an Egyptian while trying to protect a Hebrew. Moses was exiled to Midian until God appeared to him at age eighty in a burning bush and commissioned him to deliver the children of Israel out of Egyptian bondage.

The Deliverance Moses returned to Egypt but was unable to convince Pharaoh to let the children of Israel go to worship God. God sent ten plagues on the land of Egypt to show Pharaoh and all Egypt that He was the Lord.

The Exodus Following the tenth plague, in which Pharaoh's own son died, Pharaoh let the children of Israel go out of Egypt. When Pharaoh realized what he had done, he changed his mind and pursued the children of Israel. God parted the Red Sea, and the Israelites crossed the Red Sea on dry ground, but Pharaoh's army was drowned when they tried to follow. The Children of Israel lived in the wilderness on their way to the Promised Land. God led the children of Israel with a pillar of cloud by day and a pillar of fire by night.

The Law While in the wilderness God gave the children of Israel the Law and the promises. The Law was to teach them how to live to please God and how to properly worship God. The promises reminded them of the blessings that would be theirs when they obeyed the Law.

The Tabernacle In addition to the Law, God gave Moses instructions on how to build the tabernacle. The tabernacle was a place of worship and sacrifice, the place where God dwelt among His people. This structure was a mobile unit that was constructed so that it could be moved along with the camp of the children of Israel.

The Twelve Spies As the children of Israel arrived at the border of the Promised Land (then called Canaan), Moses sent twelve spies into the land to bring back a report regarding the people, the cities, and the land. When the spies returned, they gave a mixed report. Ten of the spies reported that the people were too strong to be conquered, but two spies (Joshua and Caleb) encouraged the people to trust in God and enter the land. The children of Israel decided to follow the advice of the ten spies and rebelled against God, and as a result God punished them.

The Desert The punishment for rebellion was that the children of Israel wandered for forty years in the desert and all the people age twenty and older died in the desert, except Joshua and Caleb.

Joshua At the end of the forty years in the wilderness Moses died at the edge of the Promised Land. God appointed Joshua to lead the children of Israel. Joshua was a warrior.

The Promised Land As the children of Israel prepared to enter the Promised Land, God gave them three commands: **no people** were to remain, they were to make **no covenants** with the people, and they were to leave **no idols or high places** in the land. If the children of Israel failed to obey these warnings, the remaining people in the land would be a constant irritation and some of the Israelites would participate in idolatry.

The Jordan In order to enter the Promised Land, the children of Israel had to cross the Jordan River. Like the Red Sea, God miraculously dried up the river so that the people could cross on dry ground. The first city conquered in the Promised Land was Jericho.

The Judges During the lifetime of Joshua, the children of Israel conquered a great deal of the Promised Land, but not all of it. Following the death of Joshua and the elders of Joshua's time, the children of Israel began a cycle that we see throughout the book of Judges. **Rebel:** The Israelites turned away from God and began to worship false gods. **Bondage:** When they rebelled, God allowed them to go into bondage to other people and countries. **Cry Out:** After a time of bondage, the children of Israel would cry out to God and ask Him to forgive them of their sins, at which time God would send a judge. **Judge:** The judge would then teach the people the Law and show them how to live to please God. The children of Israel would obey God until that judge died, and then the cycle would begin again.

Ruth During the time of the judges we have the story of a woman named Ruth. Ruth was a widow from Moab who returned to Israel with her mother-in-law so that she could serve the God of Israel. Ruth settled in Bethlehem and married an Israelite named Boaz.

Samuel Samuel was dedicated to the service of the Lord as a child. Samuel was the last judge of Israel and also served in the role of prophet to Israel. Samuel anointed the first two kings of Israel, Saul and David.

Saul During the time of Samuel, the Israelites cried out for a king so that they would be like other nations. Through Samuel God chose Saul as the first king of Israel. King Saul began his reign by serving God but soon afterwards turned away from following God. Saul had an unfaithful attitude towards God.

David God chose David as the second king of Israel. David is known as "a man after God's own heart." Although David sinned, he repented and was faithful to God throughout his lifetime. Our third indication of who the Messiah would be is found in the promise that God made to David: the Christ would be (1) born of woman, (2) born of the line of Abraham and (3) born of the line of David.

Solomon Solomon was the son of King David and was the third king of Israel. Under Solomon, Israel expanded its borders to encompass more land than at any other point in its history. When Solomon grew older, his many wives turned his heart from serving the one true God of Israel to serving and worshipping idols. Solomon, unlike his father David, grew to have a rebellious heart towards God.

First Temple While Solomon reigned he built the first temple. The temple replaced the Tabernacle as the central place of worship and sacrifice for all of Israel. The temple was built in Jerusalem and was the place where God dwelt among His people.

The Divided Kingdom Because of Solomon's sins, the kingdom of Israel was divided into two countries, Israel and Judah, during the reign of Rehoboam, Solomon's son.

The Prophets During the time of the kings and the divided kingdom, God sent prophets to the kings, cities, and countries with a message from God. God never judged a king, city, or country without first warning them of the coming judgment and giving them an opportunity to repent and return to the ways of the Lord.

Israel The country of Israel consisted of ten tribes: Rueben, Gad, Manasseh, Simeon, Ephraim, Dan, Naphtali, Asher, Zebulun, and Issachar.

Kings of Israel Israel had nineteen kings, all of whom did evil before the Lord.

Captivity of Israel Despite the warning sent from God through the prophets, the kings and people of Israel continued in their sinful ways. God sent Israel into captivity under the Assyrians, who deported and spread the tribes of Israel throughout the Assyrian kingdom. God promised Israel that one day He would bring them from the north, from the south, from the east, and from the west back to their land. We are just beginning to see this promise fulfilled. We place the three questions marks above the arrows coming out of Assyria to indicate that the time of Israel's captivity is unknown.

Judah The country of Judah consisted of the two tribes: Judah and Benjamin.

Kings of Judah Judah had twenty kings: eleven did evil before the Lord, seven did what was right before the Lord, and two did both good and evil before the Lord.

Captivity of Judah Judah failed to learn from what happened to Israel, and Babylon took Israel captive in 586 B.C. God promised Judah that they would be in captivity for seventy years, and then He would return them to their land. We place the "seventy years" above the arrows going into Babylon to indicate that the time of Judah's captivity would be seventy years.

Daniel Daniel was taken as a captive from Judah to Babylon. Daniel was faithful to God even when his faith was tested while in captivity. We know from Scripture that Daniel was a praying man. Daniel served four kings while in Babylon.

Second Temple When the seventy years of captivity in Babylon were complete, Zerubbabel led the first of three groups of captives back to Israel. Under the leadership of Zerubbabel, the first group of returning captives rebuilt the temple.

Esther During this time we have the story of Esther. Esther was a young Jewish woman who became queen of Persia. After becoming queen, she learned of a plot to kill all the Jews in the kingdom. Through her bravery she was able to save her people from death.

Ezra The second group of captives from Babylon returned with Ezra. Ezra was a priest and teacher of the Law who taught the people in Israel how to serve God.

Nehemiah The third group of captives from Babylon returned with Nehemiah. Under the leadership of Nehemiah, the walls and gates around Jerusalem were rebuilt.

400 Silent Years Nehemiah's rebuilding of the walls and gates around Jerusalem was the last chronological event of the Old Testament. The first recorded event of the New Testament takes place approximately 400 years after Nehemiah. Although this intertestamental period is often called the "silent years," it does not mean that God was not active among His people. During this time God continued to prepare His people and the world for the coming of the Messiah.

Old Testament Timeline

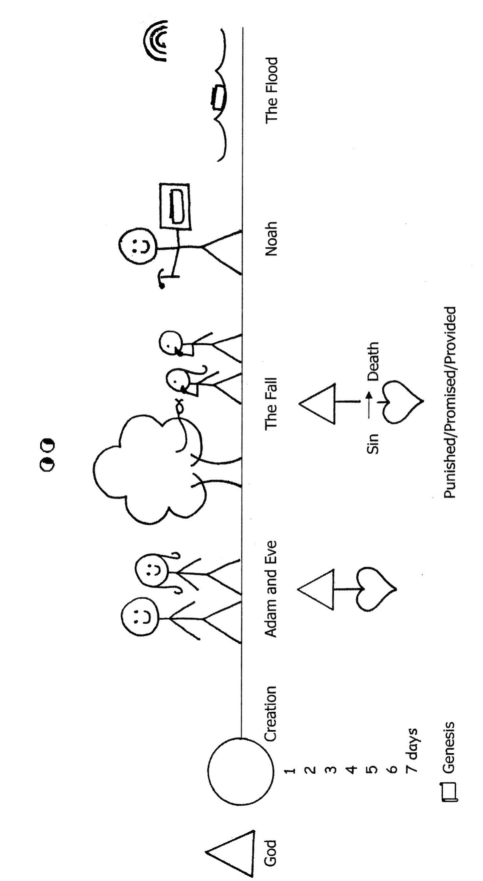

God

Creation
1
2
3
4
5
6
7 days

Genesis

Adam and Eve

The Fall

Sin → Death

Punished/Promised/Provided

Noah

The Flood

7

SP 3

Grapevine Studies
Old Testament

Old Testament Timeline

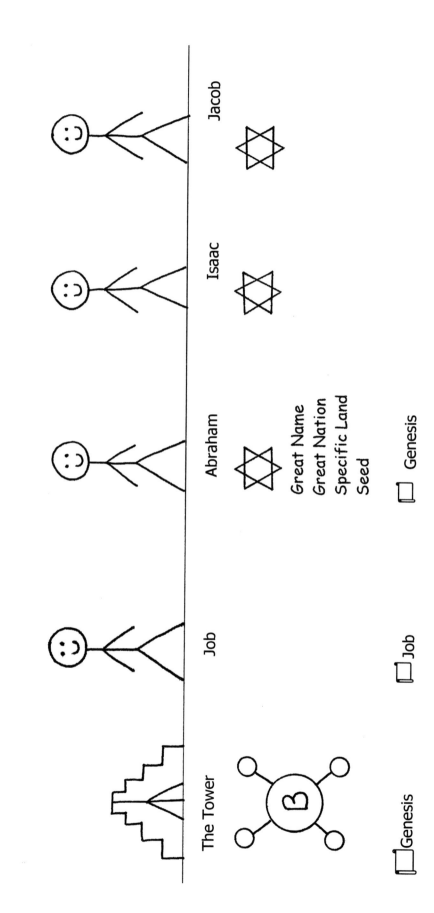

The Tower

Job

Abraham

Isaac

Jacob

Great Name
Great Nation
Specific Land
Seed

Genesis

Job

Genesis

Grapevine Studies
Old Testament

Old Testament Timeline

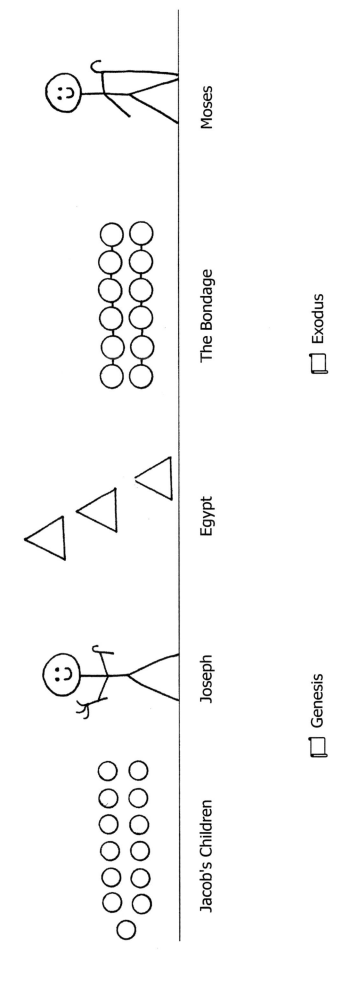

| Jacob's Children | Joseph | Egypt | The Bondage | Moses |

☐ Genesis   ☐ Exodus

SP 5

Old Testament Timeline

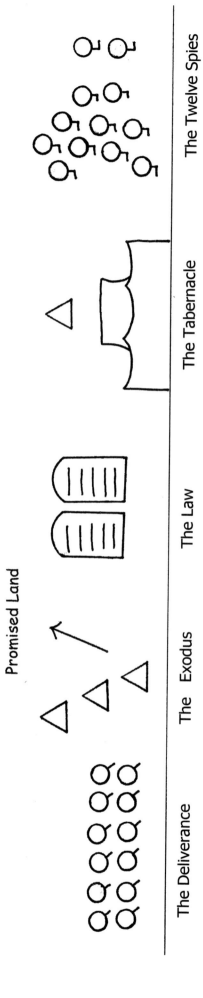

Promised Land

| The Deliverance | The Exodus | The Law | The Tabernacle | The Twelve Spies |

Exodus   Leviticus, Numbers, Deuteronomy

SP 6

Old Testament Timeline

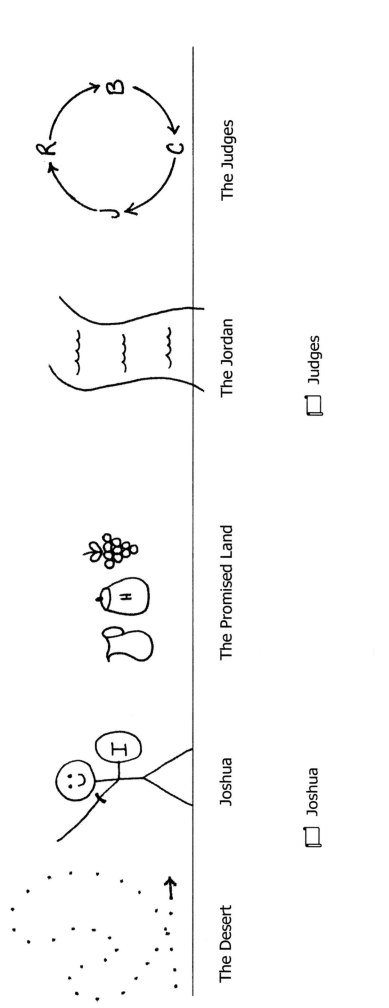

The Desert   Joshua   The Promised Land   The Jordan   The Judges

☐ Joshua   ☐ Judges

SP 7

Old Testament Timeline

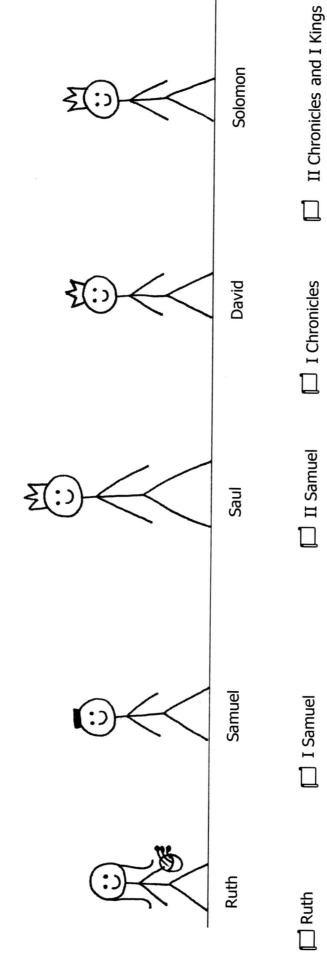

Ruth

Samuel

Saul

David

Solomon

☐ Ruth

☐ I Samuel

☐ II Samuel

☐ I Chronicles

☐ Psalms

☐ II Chronicles and I Kings

☐ Proverbs, Ecclesiastes, Song of Solomon

SP 8

12

Old Testament Timeline

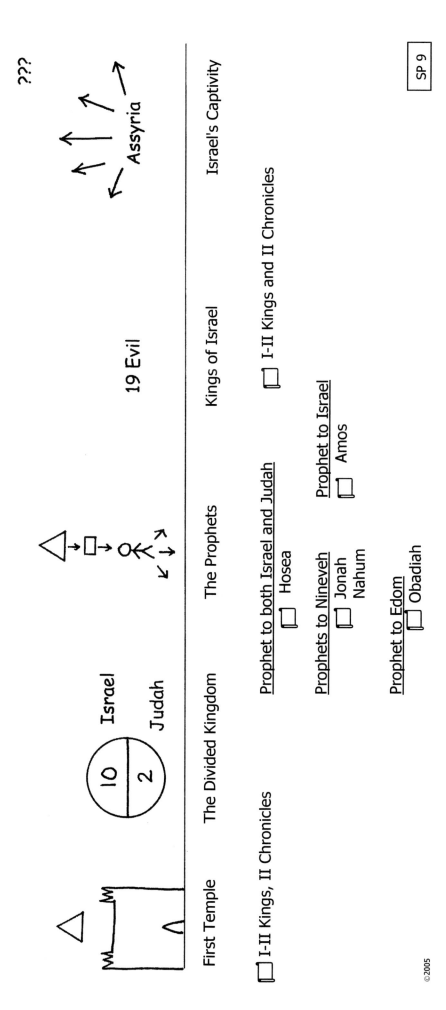

First Temple

The Divided Kingdom

The Prophets

Kings of Israel

Israel's Captivity

Israel

Judah

10

2

19 Evil

Assyria

???

☐ I-II Kings, II Chronicles

Prophet to both Israel and Judah
  ☐ Hosea

Prophets to Nineveh
  ☐ Jonah
    Nahum

Prophet to Edom
  ☐ Obadiah

Prophet to Israel
  ☐ Amos

☐ I-II Kings and II Chronicles

SP 9

Grapevine Studies
Old Testament

Old Testament Timeline

70 Years

Babylon

11 Evil
7 Good
2 Both

Second Temple

Daniel

Ezra

Judah's Captivity

I-II Kings and II Chronicles

Lamentations

Kings of Judah

Prophets to Judah
Isaiah
Jeremiah
Ezekiel
Joel
Micah
Habakkuk
Zephaniah
Haggai
Zechariah
Malachi

SP 10

14

Grapevine Studies
Old Testament

Old Testament Timeline

O.T.   N.T.

400 Years

400 Silent Years

Esther   Ezra   Nehemiah

☐ Esther   ☐ Ezra   ☐ Ezra and Nehemiah

15

SP 11

Section 2 Goals and Key Points

CREATION

The goal of this lesson is to establish the fact that in the beginning God created all things in six days and rested on the seventh day.

Key points:
- God created in the beginning.
- God created all things, including man.
- God created in six days and rested on the seventh day.

ADAM AND EVE

The goal of this lesson is to establish that the first man created was Adam, the first woman was Eve, and at their creation the relationship they had with God was complete and unbroken. In this lesson it is important to note that God formed Adam differently than any other part of creation. Adam was also given work, tending the garden and naming the beasts of the field and birds of the air. After the naming of the animals, Adam realized he did not have a helper. Eve was created out of Adam, and God gave Eve to Adam as his wife.

Key Points:
- Adam was the first man created.
- God gave Adam a job: to tend the Garden of Eden.
- God brought animals to Adam for him to name, and at that time Adam realized that he had no helper.
- From Adam God created Eve, and God gave Eve to Adam as his wife.
- At creation the relationship between God and man was complete and unbroken.

THE FALL

The goal of this lesson is to establish that Adam and Eve sinned when they disobeyed God and ate the forbidden fruit. This sin caused the relationship between man and God to be broken. Teachers will need to introduce and explain what sin is and how it affects our relationship to God and who the serpent was and is.

Key Points:
- Satan deceived Eve, and she ate from the tree of the knowledge of good and evil, and then Adam ate.
- The sin of Adam and Eve was disobedience to God.

Key Points (cont.):
- Because of sin, the relationship between God and man was changed and broken.
- This sin had both short-term effects (removal from the garden) and long-term consequences (death, broken relationship with God, and the curses).
- It is here that we are introduced to the concept that sin is covered only with a blood sacrifice. God killed an animal, shedding its blood to provide coverings for Adam and Eve as they left the garden.

NOAH AND THE FLOOD

The goal of this lesson is to establish the reasons for the Flood and the magnitude of the Flood. It is important to note how sin affected the family of Adam and Eve.

Key Points:
- Adam and Eve had many sons and daughters.
- Adam's sin affected his children.
- Cain murdered Abel.
- Noah lived ten generations after Adam.
- The men of Noah's day were thoroughly wicked and very violent.
- Noah was a righteous man who found favor with God.
- Noah was instructed by God to build an ark to save his family, two of every kind of unclean animal, and seven of every kind of clean animal.
- The Flood came and covered the entire earth.

THE TOWER OF BABEL

The goal of this lesson is for the students to understand that the Tower of Babel was built in direct disobedience to God's command and that as a result, God confused their language, which caused the people to scatter.

Key Points:
- The first thing Noah and his family did after leaving the ark was to sacrifice and worship God.
- God promised that He would never again flood the earth, and the sign of that promise was the rainbow.
- After leaving the ark God told the people to scatter and fill the earth.
- After the several generations, the number of people had grown, and they decided to gather together and build a city and a tower.
- Because of the people's disobedience, God confused the language, causing them to scatter throughout the earth.

Level 4

CREATION

Today you will introduce your students to the first of the three Bible study tools that we will use in this series, the topical Bible. The topical Bible is used to do research on a specific topic or subject. In a topical Bible, subjects are listed with their definitions and/or references so that further research on that subject can be done easily. Today we will examine the different ways the topical Bible can be used. The italicized words are the ones your students will look up.

Teachers: We have given page numbers for the answers that can be found in the Nave's, Compact Topical Bible, (Published by Zondervan), but due to copyright restrictions we are unable to print the answers.

Topical Bible

1. Give three ways the *Creator* is referred to in the Bible.

Nave's, page105

2. Give the meaning of the names *Adam* and *Eve* (found in parentheses).

Nave's, page 7, 144

3. Give the four references about God creating *light.* (The Scriptures will be found after the word "Created.")

Genesis 1:3-5, Psalm 74:16, Isaiah 45:7, II Corinthians 4:6 (Nave's, page 293)

SP 13

CREATION

Background Bible Reading: Genesis 1-2
Time Frame: In the beginning

In the beginning God: *God gave us this record of His work so that we would know that He is the Creator of all. This is "His Story," the history of the world. Throughout the Bible we will see God at work in the lives of men and women throughout history. Let's start at the beginning. In the beginning who? God was there before anything was created, and He created all that is out of nothing.*

beginning, created   *Draw a purple triangle for God.*

Days of Creation

Day 1: *God established when Creation took place "in the beginning." God created by speaking the word ("God said..."), and it was so. God created light and defined what day and night mean.*

light, day, night   *Draw light and darkness.*

Day 2: *"Waters above" refers to the sky.*

---

firmament, waters above, waters below   *Draw waters above and below.*

Day 3: *God gathered the waters together, calling them "seas," and He let the dry land appear, calling it "earth." God created an orderly world with plants and trees that reproduced after their own kind.*

kind, good   *Draw land with trees and plants and the sea.*

Day 4: *God created the sun as the ruler of the day and the moon and stars as the rulers of the night. The heavenly lights mark days, years, signs, and seasons.*

Draw the sun, moon, and stars.

CREATION

Time Frame: In the beginning

Gen. 1:1

"In the beginning God..."

Days of Creation

Gen. 1:1-5

Day 1

Light, Night and Day

Gen. 1:6-8

Day 2

Division of the waters

Gen. 1:9-13

Day 3

Dry land and seas,
Plants and trees

Gen. 1:14-19

Day 4

Heavenly lights

SP 14

CREATION

Day 5: *God created the fish, sea creatures, and birds "according to their kind," and then God commanded them to be fruitful and multiply.*

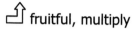 fruitful, multiply   *Draw birds in the sky, animals in the sea.*

Day 6: *God created all the land animals, according to their kind, on the sixth day. Man was the last and greatest of God's creation. Man was created in God's image and was given dominion over the rest of creation.*

---

 dominion   *Draw Adam, Eve, and a land animal.*

Day 7: *God saw all that He had created, and it was "very good." On the seventh day God rested from His work, sanctified that day, and established the pattern for our week. (Exodus 31:17)*

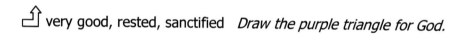 very good, rested, sanctified   *Draw the purple triangle for God.*

---

1. When did God create? *In the beginning.*
2. How did God create? *He spoke and it was so.*
3. What did God do on the first day of the creation week? *He created light, night, and day.*
4. What did God do on the second day of the creation week? *He divided the waters above from the waters below.*
5. What did God do on the third day of the creation week? *He created dry land and seas, plants, and trees.*
6. What did God do on the fourth day of the creation week? *He created heavenly lights: sun, moon, and stars.*
7. What did God do on the fifth day of the creation week? *He created fish, sea creatures, and birds.*
8. What did God do on the sixth day of the creation week? *He created land animals and man.*
9. What did God do on the seventh day of the creation week? *God rested.*
10. What do we learn about God from these verses? *God is the Creator of all things.*

©2005

Gen. 1:20-23

Day 5

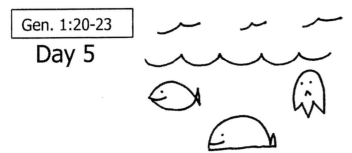

Fish, sea creatures and birds

Gen. 1:24-27

Day 6

Land animals, man & woman

Gen. 1:31, 2:1-3

Day 7

God rested

Lesson Review

1. When did God create?
2. How did God create?
3. What did God do on the first day of the creation week?
4. What did God do on the second day of the creation week?
5. What did God do on the third day of the creation week?
6. What did God do on the fourth day of the creation week?
7. What did God do on the fifth day of the creation week?
8. What did God do on the sixth day of the creation week?
9. What did God do on the seventh day of the creation week?
10. What do we learn about God from these verses?

Memory Verse: Genesis 1:1 and Genesis 1:31.

SP 15

Level 3

Create a card for Creation.

- *Day 1: Light, night and day*
- *Day 2: Division of the waters*
- *Day 3: Dry land and seas, plants, and trees*
- *Day 4: Sun, moon, and stars*
- *Day 5: Fish, sea creatures, birds*
- *Day 6: Land animals, man and woman*
- *Day 7: God rested.*

Level 4

ADAM AND EVE

Today you will introduce your students to the second of the three Bible study tools that we will use in this series, the Bible dictionary. In a Bible dictionary, subjects are listed with definitions and references so that students can have a clear understanding of the word(s) they are researching. Today we will examine the different ways the Bible dictionary can be used. The words your students will look up are italicized.

Teachers: We have given page numbers for the answers that can be found in the Zondervan's Compact Bible Dictionary, (Published by Zondervan), but due to copyright restrictions we are unable to print the answers.

Bible Dictionary

1. Give the literal meaning of the word *Eden* (the bold print in parentheses).
   Zondervan's, page 141

2. Give the first definition of the name *Eve* (found after the parentheses).
   Zondervan's, page 162

3. In what passage, besides Genesis 2:9, 22 and 24, do we find the *Tree of Life?* (The Scriptures are in the definition.)
   Zondervan's, page 592

SP 16

ADAM AND EVE

Timeline Review

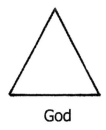

God

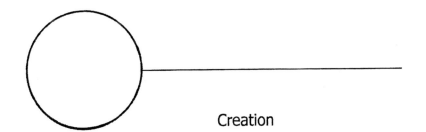

Creation

Bible Verses

Genesis 1:1

Genesis 1:31

SP 17

ADAM AND EVE

Background Bible Reading: Genesis 1-2
Time Frame: In the beginning

_____

God Formed Adam: *Adam was a special creation of God in that God formed him from the dust of the earth and then breathed into him the breath of life.*

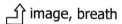 image, breath   *Draw God (triangle) breathing life into Adam.*

_____

Adam's Home and Job: *Adam lived in the Garden of Eden and his job was to tend the garden.*

 tend   *Draw Adam working in the Garden of Eden.*

_____

God Gave Adam a Command: *God gave Adam the freedom to eat from all of the trees in the Garden of Eden except one, the tree of the knowledge of good and evil. God said that in the day that Adam ate the fruit of that tree, he would surely die.*

die   *Draw God commanding Adam not to eat of the tree.*

ADAM AND EVE

Bible Verses: Genesis 2:4-24
Time Frame: In the beginning

Gen. 2:4-7

God Formed Adam

Gen. 2:15

Adam's Home and Job

Gen. 2:16-17

God Gave Adam a Command

©2005

SP 18

27

ADAM AND EVE

Adam Named the Animals and Found No Helper: *God brought the animals of the field and the birds to Adam to see what he would name them. As Adam looked at all of the animals, he realized that there was nothing in creation comparable to him, no one to be his helper.*

 helper   *Draw Adam naming male and female birds and animals.*

God Formed Eve: *God formed Eve especially for Adam, from Adam's own body.*

 woman   *Draw God removing the rib from Adam and giving it to Eve.*

God Gave Adam a Wife: *Here God defined marriage: it comes when a man leaves his father and mother and joins together with his wife to form a new family unit. God gave Eve to Adam, and together they formed the first family.*

Draw God over Adam and Eve.

1. How was Adam created different from all of the rest of creation? *God formed Adam in His own image and breathed into Adam the breath of life.*
2. Where did Adam live? *The Garden of Eden.*
3. What was Adam's job in the garden? *To tend the garden.*
4. Who named the animals of the field and the birds? *Adam.*
5. What command did God give to Adam? *Do not eat from the tree of the knowledge of good and evil.*
6. How was Eve created? *From the side of Adam.*
7. When did God create Eve? *When Adam realized that he had no suitable helper.*
8. When was marriage established? *When God gave Eve to Adam on the sixth day.*
9. What do we learn about God from these verses? *God is the creator of man, woman, and marriage.*

©2005

Gen. 2:19-20

Adam Named the Animals and Found No Helper

Gen. 2:18, 21, 22a

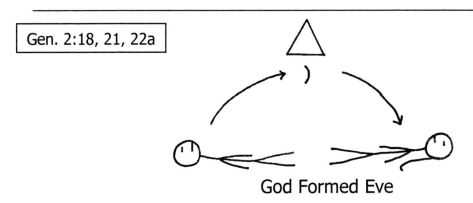

God Formed Eve

Gen. 2:22b-25

God Gave Adam a Wife

Lesson Review

1. How was Adam created different from all of the rest of creation?
2. Where did Adam live?
3. What was Adam's job in the garden?
4. Who named the animals of the field and the birds?
5. What command did God give to Adam?
6. How was Eve created?
7. When did God create Eve?
8. When was marriage established?
9. What do we learn about God from these verses?

Memory Verse: Genesis 2:7

SP 19

Level 3

Create a card for Adam and Eve.

- *The first man and woman were Adam and Eve.*
- *God created man and woman on the sixth day.*
- *At creation man's relationship to God was perfect.*
- *Adam's job was to tend the garden.*
- *Adam named the birds and the animals of the field.*
- *Eve was created from Adam.*
- *Eve was Adam's wife.*

Level 4

THE FALL

Today you will introduce your students to the third of the three Bible study tools that we will use in this series, the concordance. In a concordance, words are listed with their Biblical references and a small portion of Scripture surrounding that word. This tool is designed to give student quick access to passages they are researching. Today we will examine the different ways a concordance can be used. The words your students will look up are italicized.

Teachers: We have given page numbers for the answers that can be found in the Cruden's Compact Concordance, (Published by Zondervan), but due to copyright restrictions we are unable to print the answers.

Concordance

1. What is the first reference to *serpent* in the Bible?

    Genesis 3:1 (Cruden's, page 434)

2. Give the reference for *fig* leaves used as covering for Adam and Eve.

    Genesis 3:7 (Cruden's, page 172)

3. How many times is the word *skins* found in the Bible?

    7 (Cruden's, page 452)

4. Give the reference for "I will put *enmity* between you and the woman...."

    Genesis 3:15 (Cruden's, page 144)

SP 20

THE FALL

Timeline Review

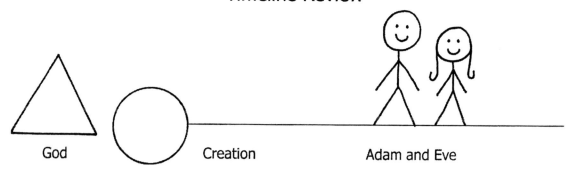

God   Creation   Adam and Eve

Bible Verses

Genesis 2:7

Genesis 1:1

Genesis 1:31

SP 21

THE FALL

Background Bible Reading: Genesis 1-3
Time Frame: After Creation

The Serpent Talked to Eve: *The serpent questioned God's command and focused on Eve's desire for the fruit.*

 serpent   *Draw the tree with the serpent talking to Eve.*

Eve Ate the Fruit: *Eve believed the serpent, followed her own desire, and ate the forbidden fruit (the type of fruit is unknown).*

 fruit   *Draw Eve eating the forbidden fruit.*

Eve Gave Adam the Fruit: *Eve gave Adam the forbidden fruit, and he too disobeyed (sinned against) God and ate. At this point, death entered into the world as a result of their sin of disobedience.*

Draw Eve giving the forbidden fruit to Adam.

Adam and Eve Hid from God: *Adam and Eve tried to hide from God by covering themselves with fig leaves. When God came to the garden, Adam and Eve were hiding from Him.*

Draw Adam and Eve hiding from God.

God Questioned Adam and Eve: *God knew that Adam and Eve had eaten the forbidden fruit but He still questioned them. Adam blamed Eve and Eve blamed the serpent.*

Draw God questioning Adam and Eve while each of them blaming someone else.

THE FALL

Bible Verses: Genesis 3:1-24
Time Frame: After Creation

Gen. 3:1-6

The Serpent Talked to Eve   Eve Ate the Fruit

Gen. 3:6-8

Eve Gave Adam the Fruit   Adam and Eve Hid from God

Gen. 3:9-13

God Questioned Adam and Eve

SP 22

THE FALL

The Punishments for Their Sins: *God had warned Adam that if he ate of the forbidden fruit he would die. The consequences that Adam faced were: his relationship with God changed, Adam's physical body began to age and he eventually died, and God drove Adam and Eve out of the Garden of Eden.*

The Serpent: *Complete chart on the next page.*

The Woman: *Complete chart on the next page.*

The Man: *Complete chart on the next page.*

 cursed, seed

---

Although God had to **punish** *their sin, God also gave them a* **promise.**
The Promise: *The promise was that one day the seed of woman would come. This seed would be a man, the Messiah, born of woman, who would crush the serpent and restore man's relationship with God.*

 enmity, bruise   *Draw the purple triangle with the Messiah bridging the gap to man's heart.*

The Provision: *God provided the first animal sacrifice for Adam and Eve, providing them with coverings as they left the Garden of Eden.*

 cherubim   *Draw Adam and Eve leaving the garden and the angel guarding Eden.*

---

1. Who talked to Eve about eating the forbidden fruit? *The serpent.*
2. How did Adam and Eve sin? *By eating the fruit.*
3. What was the sin that Adam and Eve committed? *They disobeyed God's command.*
4. What did they do after they had sinned? *They sewed fig leaves together and hid from God.*
5. What were the consequences of their sin? *See chart on the next page.*
6. What is the promise found in Genesis 3:15? *One day the seed of woman, the Messiah, would come and restore man's relationship to God.*
7. What immediate provision did God make for Adam and Eve? *God provided coverings for Adam and Eve as they left the Garden of Eden.*
8. What do we learn about God from these verses? *God does punish sin, but He provides for us even when we sin.*

Gen. 3:14-19

The Serpent

- *Cursed more than any animal*
- *Crawl on belly*
- *The seed of woman would crush the serpent's head*

The Woman

- *Pain in childbirth*
- *Desire will be for her husband*
- *Man will be head of the woman*

The Man

- *Cursed is the ground, with thorns and thistles*
- *By hard work man would eat*

The Punishments for Their Sins

Gen. 3:15

Gen. 3:20-24

Eden

Messiah

The Promise

The Provision

Lesson Review

1. Who talked to Eve about eating the forbidden fruit?
2. How did Adam and Eve sin?
3. What was the sin that Adam and Eve committed?
4. What did they do after they had sinned?
5. What were the consequences of their sin?
6. What is the promise found in Genesis 3:15?
7. What immediate provision did God make for Adam and Eve?
8. What do we learn about God from these verses?

Memory Verse: Genesis 3:15

SP 23

Level 3

Create a card for The Fall.

- *God told Adam not to eat from the tree of the knowledge of good and evil.*
- *The serpent deceived Eve into eating the forbidden fruit.*
- *Adam sinned when he ate the forbidden fruit.*
- *When Adam sinned, death came into creation and man's relationship to God was broken.*
- *God punished Adam, Eve, and the serpent for their sin.*
- *God provided coats of skin for Adam and Eve as they left the garden.*
- *God promised Adam and Eve that one day a Messiah would come who would restore man's relationship to God.*

Level 4

NOAH AND THE FLOOD

Topical Bible

Give some of the Biblical definitions for w*alking with God*.

Nave's, page 507

Bible Dictionary

What is a *cubit*?

Zondervan's, pages 120, 605

Concordance

How often is *flood* referred to in the Bible?

35 times (Cruden's, page 179)

Quest Question

Was the Flood of Noah a worldwide flood? Give your reasons.

Yes, Genesis 7:19-20 referring to the mountains being covered. Genesis 9:11 and 13 refer to God's promise never to destroy the earth with a flood again.

SP 24

NOAH AND THE FLOOD

Timeline Review

Creation   Adam and Eve   The Fall

Bible Verses

Genesis 3:15

Genesis 2:7

Genesis 1:1

Genesis 1:31

NOAH AND THE FLOOD

Background Bible Reading: Genesis 4-9
Time Frame: Ten generations after Adam

Adam, Eve, Cain, and Abel: *Adam and Eve had many children, but their first recorded sons were Abel and Cain.*

Draw Adam, Eve, Abel, and Cain.

Cain Murdered Abel: *When Cain and Abel grew up, they became old enough to offer sacrifices to God. Cain offered the fruit of his land to God, but God did not respect his offering and Cain became angry. Abel offered a first-born, fattened lamb to God, and God respected this offering. Because of his anger, Cain killed his brother Abel.*

respect(ed) *Draw Cain killing Abel.*

Cain Left: *After Cain murdered Abel, God commanded Cain to leave his family and move away from them. Adam and Eve continued to have children, and their children grew up, married one another, and had children. (Cain married one of his sisters and started a family, and his family also grew.)*

Draw Cain leaving.

The Men of Noah's Day: *The Bible notes the men of Noah's day were: wicked, had evil thoughts and imaginations continually, corrupt and filled with violence.*

wickedness, evil, sorry, grieved, corrupt, violence *Complete the chart on the next page.*

Noah: *Ten generations after Adam a man was born named Noah. Noah found grace in God's sight, was just, perfect, and walked with God.*

grace, just, perfect, walked with God *Complete the chart on the next page.*

©2005

38

NOAH AND THE FLOOD

Bible Verses: Genesis 4:1-7:29
Time Frame: Ten generations after Adam

Gen. 4:1-2	Gen. 4:3-8	Gen. 4:16

Adam, Eve, Cain, Abel	Cain Murdered Abel	Cain Left

Gen. 6:5-6, 11	Gen. 6:8-9
The Men of Noah's Day	Noah
• *Wicked*	• *Found grace in God's sight*
• *Evil thoughts continually*	• *Perfect*
• *Evil intentions continually*	• *Just*
• *Corrupt*	• *Walked with God*
• *Filled with violence/lawless*	

SP 26

NOAH AND THE FLOOD

God Commanded Noah to Build the Ark: *God was so displeased with man's intentions and actions that He decided to destroy all men and animals with a flood. God commanded Noah to build an ark and gave him instructions on how it was to be built.*

⬆ ark, cubits   *Draw Noah looking at plans and the finished ark with dimensions.*

Who Went into the Ark: *Noah and his wife, along with their three sons and their wives, were the only people who entered the ark and survived the Flood.*

Draw Noah's family.

What Went into the Ark: *God brought the animals to Noah; two of each kind of unclean animal and seven of each kind of clean animal and bird were taken in the ark. (The clean animals were probably used for sacrifice and food for Noah and his family when they left the ark.)*

Draw male and female animals.

The Flood: *When the Flood came, the fountains of the great deep were broken up and the windows of heaven were opened. The flooding continued for forty days and forty nights.*

⬆ fountains of the deep, windows of heaven   *Draw rain and the fountains opening.*

Covered the Whole Earth: *The Flood covered the entire earth, including the highest mountains, killing all men and animals that were not in the ark.*

⬆ prevailed   *Draw water covering even the mountains.*

1. What happened to Cain and Abel? *Cain murdered Abel, and God sent him away.*
2. Describe the men of Noah's day. *Wicked, had evil thoughts and imaginations continually, corrupt and filled with violence.*
3. Describe Noah. *Noah found grace in God's sight, was just, perfect, and walked with God.*
4. Who went on the ark? *Noah, his wife, his three sons, and their wives.*
5. What happened to those who did not go into the ark? *They died in the Flood.*
6. What animals went into the ark? *Two of each kind of unclean animal, seven of each kind of clean animal.*
7. How much of the earth was flooded? *The whole earth including the highest mountains.*
8. What do we learn about God from these verses? *God judges sin but He also protects us when we obey Him.*

©2005

Gen. 6:13-17

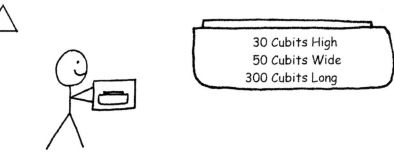

30 Cubits High
50 Cubits Wide
300 Cubits Long

God Commanded Noah to Build the Ark

Gen. 6:10, 18-22; 7:13-16

Who Went into the Ark

What Went into the Ark

Gen. 7:5-12

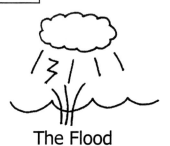

The Flood

Gen. 7:18-22

Covered the Whole Earth

Lesson Review

1. What happened to Cain and Able?
2. Describe the men of Noah's day.
3. Describe Noah.
4. Who went on the ark?
5. What happened to those who did not go into the ark?
6. What animals went into the ark?
7. How much of the earth was flooded?
8. What do we learn about God from these verses?

Memory Verse: Genesis 6:8

SP 27

Level 3

Create a card for Noah.

- *Noah found grace in the eyes of the Lord, was blameless and walked with God.*
- *The men of Noah's day were very wicked.*
- *Noah had three sons: Shem, Ham, and Japheth.*
- *God told Noah to build an ark because He was going to flood the whole earth.*
- *Noah built the ark.*
- *Noah took his wife, his sons, and their wives into the ark.*
- *God brought seven of every kind of clean animal and two of every kind of unclean animal to Noah to be put in the ark.*

Create a card for The Flood.

- *The Flood came after Noah built the ark and the people and animals had been on the Ark seven days.*
- *The Flood came as the floodgates of heaven opened and the gates of the deep were broken up.*
- *It rained for forty days and forty nights.*
- *The floodwaters covered the entire earth including the highest mountains.*

Level 4

THE TOWER OF BABEL

Topical Bible

What do you learn about the *rainbow*?

Nave's, page 398

Bible Dictionary

Give the meaning of the *Tower of Babel*?

Zondervan's, page 67

Concordance

Give the first reference to *language* in the Bible?

Genesis 11:1 (Cruden's, page 281)

Quest Question

When God gives a command, what options do we have?

To obey or disobey; either way we face the consequences of our choices.

SP 28

THE TOWER OF BABEL

Timeline Review

Adam and Eve   *The Fall*   Noah   *The Flood*

Bible Verses

Genesis 6:8

Genesis 3:15

Genesis 2:7

SP 29

THE TOWER OF BABEL

Background Bible Reading: Genesis 8-11
Time Frame: After the Flood

___

The Landing: *The waters receded off the face of the earth, and the ark landed on the mountains of Ararat.*

Draw the ark on a mountain.

___

Noah and His Family Worshipped*: After Noah, his family, and the animals had been on the ark more than a year (Gen. 7:11 and 8:13), the waters had dried up enough for them to exit the ark. The first thing recorded that the family did upon leaving the ark was to worship God by making an altar and offering sacrifices.*

altar, burnt offerings   *Draw Noah and his family worshipping at the altar.*

___

The Promise: *God promised Noah and his descendants, as well as the animals, that He would never again destroy the whole earth with a flood.*

covenant, descendants   *Draw no worldwide flood.*

___

The Sign of the Promise: *God promised man and all living creatures that He would never again flood the entire earth. As a sign of His promise, God set the rainbow in the sky.*

sign   *Draw a rainbow.*

©2005

THE TOWER OF BABEL

Bible Verses: Genesis 8:3-11:9
Time Frame: After the Flood

Gen. 8:3-4

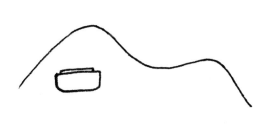

The Landing

Gen. 8:14-20

Noah and His Family Worshipped

Gen. 9:8-11

The Promise

Gen. 9:12-17

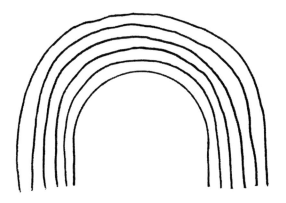

The Sign of the Promise

SP 30

©2005

THE TOWER OF BABEL

God's Command—Scatter and Fill: *God commanded man to be fruitful, multiply, and fill the earth.*

⌂ fruitful, multiply, fill   *Draw the ark and arrows indicating the command to scatter.*

The People Gathered and Built: *Instead of obeying God, the people gathered and built a city, called Babel and a tower in clear rebellion against what God had commanded them to do.*

⌂ tower   *Draw the people gathering and building a tower.*

God Confused the Language: *When God saw the city and the tower the people were building, He confused the language of the people.*

⌂ language, speech   *Draw the people confused.*

The People Were Scattered: *Since their languages were confused this forced the people to scatter. (This is the origin of ethnic people groups, language groups, tribes, etc.)*

✧ (1) Babel

⌂ Babel   *Draw a circle labeled "Babel" with four satellite circles.*

1. Where did the ark land? *On the mountains of Ararat.*
2. What did Noah and his family do after coming off the ark? *They built an altar and worshipped God.*
3. What promise did God make to man and all living creatures? *He would never again flood the whole earth.*
4. What was the sign of this promise? *The rainbow.*
5. Where did the people gather, and where did God confuse the language? *Babel.*
6. When did the people scatter? *After God confused the language.*
7. What do we learn about God from these verses? *God keeps His promises. God also wants us to obey Him and not rebel against His commands.*

©2005

46

Gen. 11:1-2, 4

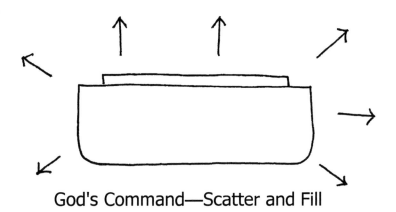

God's Command—Scatter and Fill

Gen. 11:1-2, 4

The People Gathered and Built

Gen. 11:7

God Confused the Language

Gen. 11:8-9

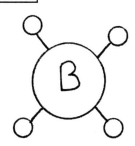

The People Were Scattered

Lesson Review

1. Where did the ark land?
2. What did Noah and his family do after coming off the ark?
3. What promise did God make to man and all living creatures?
4. What was the sign of this promise?
5. Where did the people gather, and where did God confuse the language?
6. When did the people scatter?
7. What do we learn about God from these verses?

Memory Verse: Genesis 11:9

©2005

SP 31

47

Review 1

1. When did God create all things? *In the beginning.*

2. How did God create? *He spoke and it was so.*

3. What did God do on the first day of the creation week? *He created light, night, and day.*

4. What did God do on the second day of the creation week? *He divided the waters above from the waters below.*

5. What did God do on the third day of the creation week? *He created dry land and seas, plants, and trees.*

6. What did God do on the fourth day of the creation week? *He created the heavenly lights, sun, moon, and stars.*

7. What did God do on the fifth day of the creation week? *He created fish, sea creatures, and birds.*

8. What did God do on the sixth day of the creation week? *He created land animals and man.*

9. What did God do on the seventh day of the creation week? *God rested.*

10. Recite Genesis 1:1.

11. Recite Genesis 1:31.

12. How was Adam created different from all of the rest of creation? *God formed Adam in His own image and breathed into Adam the breath of life.*

13. Where did Adam live when he was first created? *The Garden of Eden.*

14. What was Adam's job in the Garden of Eden? *To tend the garden.*

15. Who named the animals of the field and the birds? *Adam.*

16. What command did God give to Adam? *Do not eat from the tree of the knowledge of good and evil.*

17. When did God create Eve? *When Adam realized that he had no suitable helper.*

18. How was Eve created? *From the side of Adam.*

19. When was marriage established? *When God gave Eve to Adam on the sixth day.*

20. Recite Genesis 2:7.

21. Who talked to Eve about eating the forbidden fruit? *The serpent.*

22. How did Adam and Eve sin? *By eating the fruit.*

SP 32

23. What was the sin that Adam and Eve committed when they ate the forbidden fruit? *They disobeyed God's command.*

24. What did Adam and Eve do after they had sinned? *They sewed fig leaves together and hid from God.*

25. What is the promise found in Genesis 3:15? *One day the seed of woman, the Messiah, would come and restore man's relationship to God.*

26. What immediate provision did God make for Adam and Eve? *God provided coverings for Adam and Eve as they left the Garden of Eden.*

27. Recite Genesis 3:15.

28. What happened to Cain and Abel? *Cain murdered Abel, God marked Cain and sent him away.*

29. Describe the men of Noah's day. *Wicked, continually doing evil and thinking evil, corrupt and lawless.*

30. Describe Noah. *He found grace in the eyes of the Lord, walked with God, was called just and perfect.*

31. Who went on the ark? *Noah, his wife, his three sons and their wives.*

32. What happened to those who did not go into the ark? *They died in the Flood.*

33. What animals went into the ark? *Two of each kind of unclean animal, seven of each kind of clean animal.*

34. How much of the earth was flooded? *The whole earth, including the highest mountains.*

35. Recite Genesis 6:8.

36. Where did the ark land? *On the mountains of Ararat.*

37. What did Noah and his family do after coming off the ark? *They built an altar and worshipped God.*

38. What promise did God make to man and all living creatures? *He would never again flood the whole earth.*

39. What was the sign of the promise that God made to never again flood the entire earth? *The rainbow.*

40. Where did the people gather after the Flood, and where did God confuse the languages? *Babel.*

41. When did the people scatter? *After God confused the language.*

42. Recite Genesis 11:9.

SP 33

Section 3 Goals and Key Points

JOB

The goal of this lesson is for the students to understand that we, like Job, don't always understand why things are happening around us and to us. But even when we don't understand events surrounding us, we need to know that God will do nothing outside of His character, and we must never accuse God of wrongdoing.

Key Points:
- Job was a righteous man.
- Satan accused Job of following God only because God protected and blessed him.
- Job lost all his children and wealth in one day.
- Satan accused Job of following God only because God had not touched him physically.
- Job was struck with boils.
- Job had three friends who came to talk to him about what was happening to him and why.
- God spoke to Job and reminded Job of whom He is.
- Job repented and acknowledged his incomplete understanding of God.
- God blessed Job with ten more children and restored double the wealth he had lost.

ABRAHAM

The goal of this lesson is to introduce students to Abraham and the fact that God made an important covenant with Abraham.

Key Points:
- Abram was born ten generations after Noah, twenty generations after Adam.
- God made a covenant with Abram, promising to make Abram a great nation, to give him a great name, to give him a specific land, and that through his family all the families of the earth would be blessed.
- Abram had a son through his wife Hagar; Ishmael is called the "child of the flesh."
- God changed Abram's name to Abraham.
- God promised a son to Abraham and Sarah; Isaac is called the "child of promise."

ISAAC

The goal of this lesson is to show that the child promised to Abraham by God was Isaac. God made the same covenant with Isaac that He had made with Abraham.

Key Points:
- Isaac was the child promised by God to Abraham and Sarah.
- God tested Abraham's faith by telling him to offer Isaac as a sacrifice.
- God prevented Abraham from killing Isaac and provided a ram in Isaac's place.
- After Sarah died, Isaac married Rebekah.
- Isaac and Rebekah had twin sons named Esau and Jacob.
- God made the same covenant with Isaac that He had made with Abraham.

JACOB

The goal of this lesson is to look at how Jacob not only received the blessings of his father but also the blessings of God. God made the same covenant with Jacob that He had made with Abraham and Isaac.

Key Points:
- Jacob was one of the twin sons born to Isaac and Rebekah; the other was Esau.
- At Rebekah's prompting, Jacob deceived his father into blessing him instead of Esau.
- Esau hated Jacob, and because of this hatred Jacob left and stayed with his uncle, Laban, in Hebron.
- Jacob worked for Laban for many years and married Laban's daughters, Leah and Rachel.
- Jacob left Hebron and returned to his homeland in peace with four wives, thirteen children, his servants, and livestock.
- God made the same covenant with Jacob that He had made with Abraham and Isaac.

JOSEPH THE SLAVE

The goal of this lesson is to show that Joseph was favored by his father above his brothers, which resulted in their hatred toward him. As a result of their hatred, they sold him as a slave to Egypt.

Key Points:
- Joseph was the firstborn son of Rachel, Jacob's favorite wife.
- Joseph's brothers were jealous of him.
- When Joseph went to see his brothers in the field, they plotted to kill him.
- Instead of killing Joseph, they sold him as a slave.

JOSEPH THE RULER

The goal of this lesson is to show that Joseph understood that he was sent to Egypt by God in order to save his family and others from the famine.

Key Points:
- Pharaoh had a dream, and God told Joseph the meaning of Pharaoh's dream; as a result Joseph was promoted to second in command of all of Egypt.
- Joseph tested his brothers before revealing to them who he was.
- Jacob and all the rest of his family moved to Egypt to be with Joseph.
- Before Joseph died he made his family promise that when the children of Israel returned to the Promised Land, they would take his bones with them.

Level 3

Add to the card for The Flood.
- *After the Flood God promised that He would never again flood the entire earth. The sign of this promise wais the rainbow.*

Create a card for The Tower of Babel.
- *After the Flood God told Noah and his family to scatter and fill the earth.*
- *Instead of scattering, men gathered after the Flood and built a city named Babel.*
- *In Babel they built a tower that displeased God.*
- *At Babel God confused the language of the whole earth, and the people scattered.*

Level 4

JOB

Topical Bible

If we wanted to know the trials *Job* suffered, in what portion of Scripture would we look?

Job 1:13-19, 2:7-10 (Nave's, page 266)

Bible Dictionary

Give the meaning of the name *Satan* and one other name or description.

Zondervan's, page 526

Concordance

How often is *Satan* mentioned in the Bible?

Cruden's, page 421

Quest Question

Does Satan have access to God?

Yes. Job 1:6, 2:7; Revelation 12:10

SP 34

JOB

Timeline Review

The Fall Noah The Flood *The Tower*

Bible Verses

Genesis 11:9

Genesis 6:8

Genesis 3:15

SP 35

JOB

Background Bible Reading: The Book of Job
Time Frame: Unknown

Job: *Job was blameless and upright, he feared God and shunned evil. Job had seven sons, three daughters, and great wealth: 7,000 sheep, 3,000 camels, 500 yoke of oxen, 500 female donkeys.*

⤒ blameless, upright, feared, shunned   *Draw Job, his children, and his animals.*

God and Satan: *The sons of God came and presented themselves before God, and Satan appeared with them. God asked Satan to consider His servant Job. Satan responded by accusing Job of serving God only because God had blessed and protected him. Satan was given authority to test Job, but he was not allowed to touch Job's body.*

⤒ sons of God, Satan, considered, hedge, curse, presence   *Draw Satan before God.*

Job Lost Everything: *In one day Job lost all of his children, all his sheep, camels, oxen, and donkeys, and many of his servants. Job's response was one of grief and worship. He acknowledged that "the Lord gave, and the Lord has taken away." In Job's great loss, he did not sin or charge God with any wrongdoing.*

⤒ sin, charge, wrong   *Draw ten graves and Job grieving but without sin.*

God and Satan: *After Job's great loss, Satan again appeared in the presence of God. God asked Satan to reconsider His servant Job. Satan requested permission to further test Job, and God allowed Satan to afflict Job physically but not to kill him.*

⤒ integrity, incited   *Draw Satan before God's throne pointing to Job.*
©2005

JOB

Bible Verses: The Book of Job
Time Frame: Unknown

Job 1:1-5

Job

7 Sons

3 Daughters

7,000   3,000

500   500

Job

Job 1:6-12

God and Satan

Job 1:13-22

Job Lost Everything

Job 2:1-6

God and Satan

SP 36

JOB

Job Was Struck with Boils: *Satan afflicted Job with painful boils, and Job sat in ashes and scraped himself with potsherds. Job was faithful to God even when his wife encouraged him to curse God.*

⇧ boils, potsherds   *Draw Job with boils.*

Job's Friends: *Job's three friends came to console him and when they had come near they were struck by the severity of Job's condition. For seven days and nights they sat in silence with him because they saw that his suffering was very great.*

Draw Job with his three friends.

God Challenged Job: *Job and his friends had a lengthy discussion about the reason why Job was suffering. After much accusation and defense, God spoke to Job. God told Job of His mighty acts and His sovereignty. Job repented and acknowledged his incomplete understanding of God.*

⇧ repent   *Draw God questioning Job.*

God Restored Job: *The Lord restored Job after he prayed for his friends. God gave Job seven more sons, and three beautiful daughters. God also restored to Job twice as much as before: 14,000 sheep, 6,000 camels, 1,000 yoke of oxen, and 1,000 female donkeys.*

⇧ accepted, restored   *Draw Job's restored children and animals.*

1. What was Job like? *Blameless, upright, feared God, and shunned evil.*
2. How many sons and daughters did Job have altogether? *Fourteen sons and six daughters.*
3. What did Job own altogether? *21,000 sheep, 9,000 camels, 1,500 yoke of oxen, 1,500 donkeys.*
4. Who appeared before God and tested Job's faith? *Satan.*
5. When Job lost everything, how did he respond? *He grieved but did not sin or accuse God of wrongdoing.*
6. Who came to visit Job? *His three friends: Eliphaz, Bildad, and Zophar.*
7. When God challenged Job what did God show him? *That God alone is all-powerful and that Job had an incomplete knowledge of Him.*
8. What did God give Job? *More sons and daughters and twice as much wealth as before.*
9. What do we learn about God from these verses? *God is sovereign, and although we often do not understand why things are happening to us, we should be like Job and never accuse God of wrongdoing.*

Job 2:7-10

Job 2:11-13

Job Was Struck with Boils

Job's Friends

Job 38:1-7; 42:1-6

Job 42:9-17

7 sons

3 daughters

14,000

6,000

1,000

1,000

God Challenged Job

God Restored Job

Lesson Review

1. What was Job like?
2. How many sons and daughters did Job have altogether?
3. What did Job own altogether?
4. Who appeared before God and tested Job's faith?
5. When Job lost everything, how did he respond?
6. Who came to visit Job?
7. When God challenged Job, what did God show him?
8. What did God give Job?
9. What do we learn about God from these verses?

Memory Verse: Job 1:22

SP 37

Level 3

Create a card for Job.
- *Job was blameless, upright, and feared God.*
- *Satan asked to test Job.*
- *God allowed Satan to test Job.*
- *Job lost all his children and wealth in one day.*
- *Job was afflicted with boils.*
- *Even with all the bad things that happened to Job, Job did not accuse God of wrongdoing.*
- *God talked to Job, and Job repented.*
- *God restored to Job seven sons, three daughters and twice the wealth he had in the beginning.*

Level 4

ABRAHAM

Topical Bible

Give three facts about *Abraham*.

Nave's, page 4

Bible Dictionary

Give the meaning of the names *Abraham* and *Sarah*.

Zondervan's, pages 15, 525

Concordance

If you needed to determine how *Isaac* received his name, what passages would you look up?

Genesis 17:19; 21:3, 12 (Cruden's, page 260)

Quest Question

How does the promise God gave in Genesis 3:15 relate to the promise that God gave Abraham in Genesis 12:1-7?

God told Abraham that the man, the "seed of woman" promised in Genesis 3, would be born in his family line.

SP 38

ABRAHAM

Timeline Review

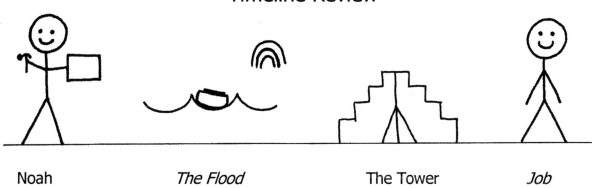

Noah   *The Flood*   The Tower   *Job*

Bible Verses

Job 1:22

Genesis 11:9

Genesis 6:8

SP 39

ABRAHAM

Background Bible Reading: Genesis 12-23
Time Frame: Ten generations after Noah

Abraham's Family: *There are ten generations between Adam and Noah. Shem is Noah's son. There are ten generations between Noah and Abraham. Terah was Abraham's father.*

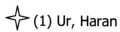 (1) Ur, Haran   *List the genealogy of Abraham.*

The Promise: *God spoke to Abram and commanded him to leave his home and family to go to the land that God would show him. God promised to make Abram a great nation, to give him a great name, to give him a specific land, and that through his family all the families of the earth would be blessed.*

 blessed   *Draw God and the promise being given to Abram.*

Hagar Ran Away: *Sarai, who was barren, convinced Abram to marry her Egyptian handmaiden, Hagar, in order to have a son. Trouble began between Sarai and Hagar soon after Abram married Hagar and she became pregnant. Sarai treated Hagar so badly that Hagar ran away to the desert. The desert was too hard for Hagar to cross, and it was there that the angel of the Lord met her and gave her promises regarding the son, whom she would bear, Ishmael. In the desert Hagar called God "The God Who Sees."*

 (1) Hebron, Canaan, Egypt

 maidservant, Hagar, Ishmael   *Draw Hagar running away.*

Ishmael Was Born: *After returning home to Abram, Hagar had a son. Abram named him Ishmael as the angel had instructed. Abram was eighty-six years old at the time Ishmael was born.*

Draw Abram, Hagar, and baby Ishmael.

ABRAHAM

Bible Verses: Genesis 12:1-23:20
Time Frame: Ten generations after Noah

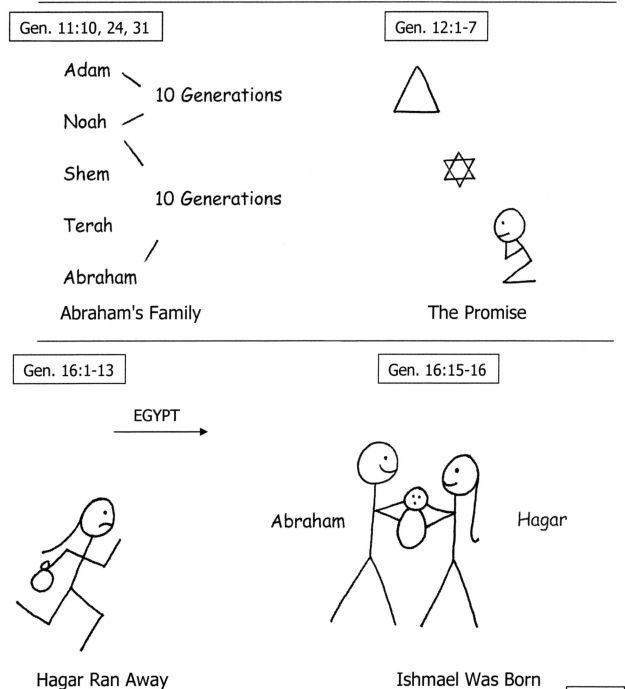

Gen. 11:10, 24, 31

Adam
10 Generations
Noah

Shem
10 Generations
Terah

Abraham

Abraham's Family

Gen. 12:1-7

The Promise

Gen. 16:1-13

EGYPT

Hagar Ran Away

Gen. 16:15-16

Abraham   Hagar

Ishmael Was Born

SP 40

ABRAHAM

God Changed the Names of Abram and Sarai: *Before the child of promise was born, God changed the names of Abram and Sarai. Abram was renamed Abraham and Sarai was renamed Sarah.*

 Abram, Abraham, Sarai, Sarah   *Write the new names next to the old names.*

Isaac Was Born: *When Abraham was one hundred years old and Sarah ninety years old, Isaac, the son promised of God, was born.*

 Isaac   *Draw baby Isaac.*

Hagar and Ishmael: *Abraham sent Hagar and Ishmael away when Sarah saw Ishmael scoffing at Isaac. God reminded Abraham that Isaac was the son of promise, but that He would also make Ishmael into a great nation. Ishmael grew up and dwelt in the wilderness of Paran, where he married an Egyptian woman.*

 scoffing   *Draw Hagar and Ishmael leaving.*

Abraham's Wives and Children:

Sarah: *Isaac, Child of Promise*

Hagar: *Ishmael, Child of the Flesh*

Keturah*: Wife after Sarah's death, six children*   *Complete chart on the next page.*

1. What did God promise Abram? *To make him a great nation, to give him a great name, to give him a specific land and that through his family all the families of the earth would be blessed.*
2. Where was Hagar from, and what was her role in the family*? Hagar was from Egypt; she was the maid of Sarai and later Abram's wife.*
3. How did Hagar describe God? *The God Who Sees.*
4. Who was the child of promise? *Isaac.*
5. How old were Abraham and Sarah when Isaac was born? *Abraham 100, Sarah 90.*
6. What was the promise regarding Ishmael? *His family would grow to be a mighty nation.*
7. What was the promise regarding Isaac? *Through his family all the nations of the earth would be blessed.*
8. Who were Abraham's wives? *Sarah, Hagar, and Keturah.*
9. What do we learn about God from these verses? *God keeps His promises in His time, and He sees all that happens.*

©2005

Gen. 17:5, 15-16

Abram   ⟶   *Abraham*

Sarai   ⟶   *Sarah*

God Changed the Names of Abram and Sarai

Gen. 17:17; 21:1-5   Gen. 21:8-14, 20-21

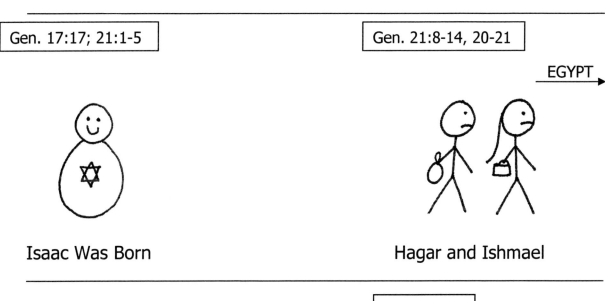

EGYPT ⟶

Isaac Was Born   Hagar and Ishmael

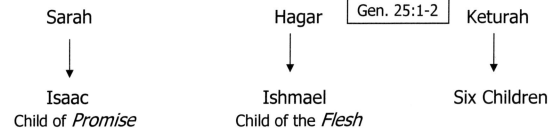

Sarah   Hagar   Gen. 25:1-2   Keturah

↓   ↓   ↓

Isaac   Ishmael   Six Children
Child of *Promise*   Child of the *Flesh*

Abraham's Wives and Children

Lesson Review

1. What did God promise Abram?
2. Where was Hagar from, and what was her role in the family?
3. How did Hagar describe God?
4. Who was the child of promise?
5. How old were Abraham and Sarah when Isaac was born?
6. What was the promise regarding Ishmael?
7. What was the promise regarding Isaac?
8. Who were Abraham's wives?
9. What do we learn about God from these verses?

Memory Verse: Genesis 22:18

SP 41

Level 3

Create a card for Abraham.

- *God promised Abraham that He would give him a:*
  1. *Great Name*
  2. *Great Nation*
  3. *Specific Land*
  4. *Seed*
- *God changed Abram's name to Abraham.*
- *Abraham was married to Sarah.*
- *God promised Abraham and Sarah a son through whom the promise would continue, this son was Isaac.*
- *Abraham had other children, Ishmael was born to Hagar, and six other children were born to Keturah.*

Level 4

ISAAC

Topical Bible

Give three facts about *Isaac*.

Nave's, page 226

Bible Dictionary

Give the meaning of the name *Isaac*.

Zondervan's, page 250

Concordance

If you were researching *burnt offerings* what are some passages you would read?

Cruden's, page 54

Quest Question

Is it ever acceptable to offer a human sacrifice to God?

No! Genesis 9:6

SP 42

ISAAC

Timeline Review

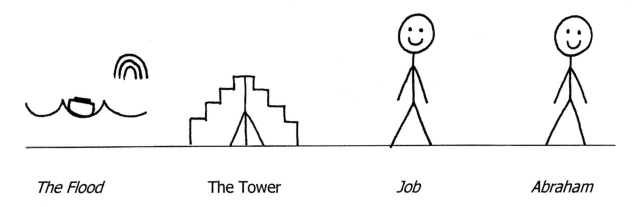

| The Flood | The Tower | Job | Abraham |

Bible Verses

Genesis 22:18

Job 1:22

Genesis 11:9

SP 43

ISAAC

Background Bible Reading: Genesis 17-25
Time Frame: Abraham

Isaac Was Born: *Isaac was born when Abraham was one hundred years old and Sarah was ninety years old. He was the son promised of God to Abraham and Sarah.*

Draw Abraham, Sarah, and baby Isaac.

The Substitutionary Sacrifice: *God tested Abraham's faith by asking him to sacrifice his promised son. Abraham's response to God's command was obedience. As Abraham obeyed God, God provided another sacrifice in place of Isaac. After offering the ram as a burnt offering, Abraham named the place "The Lord will provide."*

✧ (1) Mount Moriah

 tested, burnt offering   *Draw Abraham, Isaac, the angel, and the ram in the bushes.*

ISAAC

Bible Verses: Genesis 21:1-25:26
Time Frame: Abraham

Gen. 21:1-3

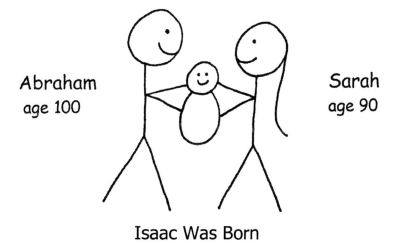

Abraham
age 100

Sarah
age 90

Isaac Was Born

Gen. 22:1-14

The Substitutionary Sacrifice

SP 44

ISAAC

Sara Died: *Sarah died, and Abraham buried her in Hebron.*

 (1) Hebron, Canaan   *Draw Sarah's grave.*

A Wife for Isaac: *When Isaac was forty years old, Abraham determined that it was time for him to marry. Abraham had his servant seek a wife for Isaac among his own people. The servant prayed, and God answered by sending Rebekah to the servant. Rebekah returned home with the servant and married Isaac.*

(1) Nahor

 meditate   *Draw the servant leading a camel, Rebekah, and Isaac praying in the field.*

Abraham Died: *At the age of 175, Abraham died after a long and full life. Abraham was buried in a cave at Machpelah, next to Sarah.*

Draw Abraham's grave.

Esau and Jacob: *Isaac pleaded with the Lord for Rebekah to conceive, and the Lord answered his prayer. Isaac was sixty years old when he and Rebekah had twin sons, Esau and Jacob.*

Esau, Jacob   *Draw Esau and Jacob.*

The Promise Was Continued to Isaac: *The promise that God made to Abraham—giving him a large family, a specific land, and that all the nations of the earth would be blessed through his family—was continued to Isaac.*

Draw God giving the promise to Isaac.

---

1. Who were Isaac's father and mother? *Abraham and Sarah.*
2. What did God tell Abraham to do to Isaac? *To sacrifice Isaac.*
3. How did God provide for Abraham in regard to sacrificing Isaac? *God stopped Abraham from sacrificing Isaac and provided a ram in his place.*
4. How did Isaac get a wife? *Abraham sent his servant to find Isaac a wife.*
5. Who was Isaac's wife? *Rebekah.*
6. How old was Isaac he married? *Forty years old.*
7. Who were Isaac's sons? *Jacob and Esau.*
8. What did God promise Isaac? *To continue the promise that He made to Abraham, giving him a large family, a specific land, and that all the nations of the earth would be blessed through his family.*
9. What do we learn about God from these verses? *God provides for those who are obedient to Him.*

©2005

Gen. 23:1-2

Gen. 24:3-4, 9-16, 46-52, 63-67

Sarah

age 40

Sarah Died

A Wife for Isaac

Gen. 25:7-10

Gen. 25:20-26

Abraham

Abraham Died

Esau and Jacob

Gen. 26:1-5

The Promise Continued to Isaac

Lesson Review

1. Who were Isaac's father and mother?
2. What did God tell Abraham to do to Isaac?
3. How did God provide for Abraham in regard to sacrificing Isaac?
4. How did Isaac get a wife?
5. Who was Isaac's wife?
6. How old was Isaac he married?
7. Who were Isaac's sons?
8. What did God promise Isaac?
9. What do we learn about God from these verses?

Memory Verse: Genesis 26:4

SP 45

Level 3

Create a card for Isaac.

- *God made to Isaac the same promise that He had made to Abraham.*

- *Isaac married Rebekah.*

- *Isaac and Rebekah had twin sons, Esau and Jacob.*

Level 4

JACOB

Topical Bible

Give three facts about *Jacob.*

Nave's, page 235

Bible Dictionary

Give the meaning of the name *Jacob.*

Zondervan's, page 263

Concordance

If you were trying to find a verse regarding *Rachel* and the fact that she could not bear children, what passages would you look up?

Genesis 30:1-2, 22 (Cruden's, page 390)

Quest Question

Should men have more than one wife?

No. Genesis 2:24; Matthew 19:4-6.

SP 46

JACOB

Timeline Review

The Tower   *Job*   Abraham   *Isaac*

Bible Verses

Genesis 26:4

Genesis 22:18

Job 1:22

JACOB

Background Bible Reading: Genesis 25-35
Time Frame: Abraham and Isaac

Esau and Jacob Were Born: *Isaac and Rebekah had twin sons, Esau and Jacob.*

Esau, Jacob   *Draw Isaac, Rebekah, Esau, and Jacob.*

Esau: *Loved by Isaac, was a cunning hunter, and a man of the field.*

man of the field

Jacob: *Loved by Rebekah, a mild man, and dwelt in the tents.*

mild man

Complete the chart on the next page.

Isaac Blessed Jacob: *Rebekah overheard a conversation between Isaac and Esau. Rebekah convinced Jacob to deceive Isaac in order for Jacob to receive the blessing of his father Isaac. Isaac blessed Jacob, and a short time later Esau returned to find his blessing bestowed upon his brother.*

bless   *Draw Isaac blessing Jacob.*

Jacob Was Sent Away: *Esau hated Jacob after Jacob received Isaac's blessing. Upon Rebekah's request, Isaac agreed to send Jacob to Rebekah's family to find a wife. Isaac again blessed Jacob, and he left and went to his uncle Laban's house in Padan Aram.*

(3) Padam Aram   *Draw Rebekah sending Jacob away.*

JACOB

Bible Verses: Genesis 25:21-35:29
Time Frame: Abraham and Isaac

Gen. 25:21-26

Isaac   Rebekah

Esau and Jacob are Born

Gen. 25:27-28

Esau	Jacob
Loved by Isaac	*Loved by Rebekah*
Hunter	*Mild man*
Man of the Field	*Dwelt in tents*

Gen. 27:1-29

Gen. 27:30-35, 41-46, 28:1-5

Padam Aram

Isaac Blessed Jacob   Jacob Was Sent Away

SP 48

JACOB

God's Promise to Jacob: *God appeared to Jacob and conferred upon Jacob the blessings of Abraham and Isaac.*

Draw God giving the promises to Jacob.

Jacob Married*: Jacob agreed to work for Laban for seven years in exchange for his daughter Rachel's hand in marriage. When the seven years were completed, Jacob was tricked into marring Rachel's older sister, Leah. Laban agreed to allow Jacob to marry Rachel, but he must work another seven years for her.*

Draw Jacob with a bride.

God Changed Jacob's Name: *Before Jacob returned to his homeland, God changed his name to Israel. The covenant that God spoke to Abraham and Isaac was then confirmed to Jacob.*

 Israel

Write "Jacob" next his new name of "Israel."

Jacob Returned Home: *After many years away from home, Jacob returned to his homeland. The reunion between Jacob and Esau was a peaceful one.*

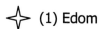 (1) Edom

Draw Jacob and Esau.

Jacob's Wives and Children: *See chart on the next page and explain why Jacob married Bilhah and Zilpah.*

Fill in the "Jacob" chart.

1. Who were Jacob's father and mother? *Isaac and Rebekah.*
2. Who was Jacob's brother? *Esau.*
3. How did Jacob get the blessing*? By making his father think he was Esau.*
4. Where did Jacob flee, and why did he go? *To Haran because Esau wanted to kill him.*
5. What was Esau's response to Jacob's return? *Esau welcomed Jacob, and there was peace between the brothers.*
6. What did God change Jacob's name to? *Israel.*
7. What did God promise Jacob? *That he would inherit the land promised to Abraham and Isaac and that through his family all the nations of the earth would be blessed.*
8. How many wives did Jacob have? *Four.*
9. How many children did Jacob have? *Thirteen.*
10. What do we learn about God from these verses? *God keeps His promises, and God is the God of Israel.*

Gen. 28:13-15

God's Promise to Jacob

Gen. 29:16-18, 20-30

Jacob Married

Gen. 35:9-12

Jacob ———▶ *Israel*

God Changed Jacob's Name

Gen. 33:1-4

Jacob Returned Home

Gen. 35:23-26

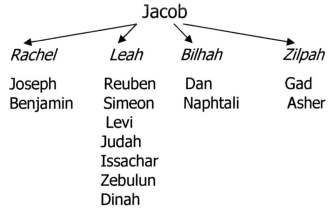

Jacob

Rachel	*Leah*	*Bilhah*	*Zilpah*
Joseph	Reuben	Dan	Gad
Benjamin	Simeon	Naphtali	Asher
	Levi		
	Judah		
	Issachar		
	Zebulun		
	Dinah		

Jacob's Wives and Children

Lesson Review

1. Who were Jacob's father and mother?
2. Who was Jacob's brother?
3. How did Jacob get the blessing?
4. Where did Jacob flee, and why did he go?
5. What was Esau's response to Jacob's return?
6. What did God change Jacob's name to?
7. What did God promise Jacob?
8. How many wives did Jacob have?
9. How many children did Jacob have?
10. What do we learn about God from these verses?

Memory Verse: Genesis 35:12

SP 49

Level 3

Create a card for Jacob.

- *God made to Jacob the same promise that He had made to Abraham and Isaac.*
- *Jacob received the blessing of Isaac instead of Esau.*
- *Jacob lived in Padam Aram for a time and worked for Laban.*
- *Jacob had four wives: Leah, Rachel, Bilhah and Zilpah.*
- *Jacob had twelve sons and one daughter.*

Level 4

JOSEPH THE SLAVE

Topical Bible

What are the two types of *servants*?

Nave's, page 436

Bible Dictionary

Give the meaning of *prison*.

Zondervan's, page 475

Concordance

What verse might contain a passage regarding Joseph being an *overseer*?

Genesis 39:4-5 (Cruden's, page 350)

Quest Question

How can we imitate Joseph when we are going through difficult times?

Joseph did his best even while in slavery, and he realized that God was with him even in the darkest hours of his life.

SP 50

JOSEPH THE SLAVE

Timeline Review

Abraham	Isaac	*Jacob*	Jacob's children

Bible Verses

Genesis 35:12

Genesis 26:4

Genesis 22:18

SP 51

JOSEPH THE SLAVE

Background Bible Reading: Genesis 37-40
Time Frame: Following Abraham, Isaac, and Jacob

Jacob Favored Joseph: *Joseph was the firstborn son of Rachel, Jacob's favorite wife, and the son of his old age. Jacob favored Joseph and even made him a special tunic of many colors. Joseph was seventeen years old when the Bible began to record the events of his life.*

 tunic   *Draw Jacob with Joseph in his colored tunic.*

Joseph's Brothers Hated Him: *Jacob sent Joseph to check on his brothers, who were out of the area tending their father's sheep. Upon seeing Joseph coming, they developed a scheme to get rid of this favored brother.*

 (2) Hebron, Shechem, Dothan
        Draw Joseph heading toward his brothers' camp as they grumble at seeing him.

Joseph Was Sold as a Slave: *Reuben convinced his brothers not to kill Joseph, so that he could return him to their father. Before Reuben could retrieve Joseph from the pit into which he had been thrown, the other brothers sold Joseph as a slave to Ishmaelite/Midianites traders.*

 (2) Egypt

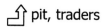 pit, traders   *Draw Joseph being led in chains to Egypt.*

Jacob Mourned for Joseph: *When the brothers returned to their father, they gave him Joseph's tunic, which they had torn and dipped into goat's blood. The brothers let Jacob believe that Joseph was dead, and Jacob went into deep mourning for Joseph. The Ishmaelite traders sold Joseph to an Egyptian man named Potiphar.*

 mourn   *Draw Jacob kneeling and crying while holding the torn tunic.*

JOSEPH THE SLAVE

Bible Verses: Genesis 37:1-40:23
Time Frame: Following Abraham, Isaac, and Jacob

Gen. 37:1-4

Jacob Favored Joseph

Gen. 37:12-14, 18-20

Joseph's Brothers Hated Him

Gen. 37:21-28

Gen. 37:31-36

17 years old

Egypt

Joseph Was Sold as a Slave

Jacob Mourned for Joseph

SP 52

JOSEPH THE SLAVE

Joseph, Overseer for Potiphar: *Joseph found favor with his master in Egypt, and God blessed Joseph and his work. Soon Joseph was overseer of the entire household of his master, Potiphar. The Lord blessed Potiphar and all he owned because of Joseph.*

 overseer

Draw Joseph with a scroll at the door of Potiphar's house.

Joseph, Overseer of the Prison: *Potiphar's wife told a lie about Joseph, and Potiphar had no choice but to send him to prison. In prison the Lord again blessed Joseph, and soon he was the overseer of the prison.*

Draw Joseph holding a scroll while in prison.

Joseph, the Chief Butler, and the Chief Baker: *The chief butler and the chief baker were thrown into prison under Joseph's care. Both these men had dreams, and the Lord used Joseph to interpret their dreams. The chief butler promised Joseph that he would remember him when he was released from prison.*

 chief butler, chief baker

Draw Joseph, the chief butler, and the chief baker talking.

1. Who was Joseph's father? *Jacob/Israel.*
2. What did Joseph's brothers do to him? *Sold him as a slave.*
3. Where was Joseph a slave (country)? *Egypt.*
4. How did Jacob respond to the reports about Joseph being dead? *He mourned greatly.*
5. What was Joseph's job in Potiphar's household? *Overseer.*
6. How did Joseph end up in prison? *Potiphar's wife told a lie about Joseph.*
7. How did God bless Joseph even while he was in prison? *He became overseer of the prison.*
8. Who were the two people that had dreams while in prison with Joseph? *The chief butler and the chief baker.*
9. What do we learn about God from these verses? *God has a plan for our lives and for those around us even when it seems as if no good can come from a bad situation. God is with us at all times.*

©2005

80

Gen. 39:1-5

Gen. 39:19-23

Potiphar

Prison

Joseph, Overseer for Potiphar

Joseph, Overseer of the Prison

Gen. 40:1-3, 7-23

Joseph, the Chief Butler, and the Chief Baker

Lesson Review

1. Who was Joseph's father?
2. What did Joseph's brothers do to him?
3. Where was Joseph a slave (country)?
4. How did Jacob respond to the reports about Joseph being dead?
5. What was Joseph's job in Potiphar's household?
6. How did Joseph end up in prison?
7. How did God bless Joseph even while he was in prison?
8. Who were the two people that had dreams while in prison with Joseph?
9. What do we learn about God from these verses?

Memory Verse: Genesis 39:2

SP 53

Level 3

Create a card for Joseph.

- *Joseph was the first son of Jacob and Rachel.*
- *Joseph was sold into slavery by his brothers when he was seventeen years old.*
- *Joseph was a slave in Egypt for thirteen years.*

Level 4

JOSEPH THE RULER

Topical Bible

What were the *magicians* of Egypt?

Nave's, page 300

Bible Dictionary

What were the four things that caused *famine*?

Zondervan's, page 170

Concordance

Give the verse referring to Joseph's *coffin.*

Genesis 50:26 (Cruden's, page 78)

Quest Question

If we love God, we will only experience "good" things and "good" times. True or False? Give your reasons why.

False; reasons will vary.

JOSEPH THE RULER

Timeline Review

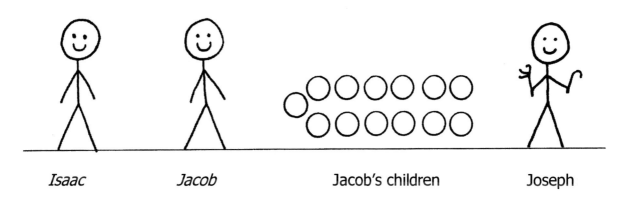

Isaac

Jacob

Jacob's children

Joseph

Bible Verses

Genesis 39:2

Genesis 35:12

Genesis 26:4

SP 55

JOSEPH THE RULER

Background Bible Reading: Genesis 41-50
Time Frame: Following Abraham, Isaac, and Jacob

Pharaoh's Two Dreams: *God sent Pharaoh two dreams to warn him of things to come. Pharaoh's wise men could not tell him what the dreams meant.*

⬆ magicians, wise men   *Draw Pharaoh on his bed dreaming of a cow and wheat.*

Joseph Before Pharaoh: *The chief butler remembered Joseph, and Joseph was called before Pharaoh. Joseph told Pharaoh that God would give him the meaning of the dreams. After hearing the dreams, Joseph told Pharaoh the meaning of the dreams and what needed to be done in Egypt to prepare for the coming famine.*

⬆ famine   *Draw Joseph before Pharaoh explaining the dreams.*

Joseph, Second in Command: *Pharaoh was impressed with the wisdom the Lord gave to Joseph, and he promoted him to second-in-command over all of Egypt. Joseph stored grain throughout all of Egypt during the years of plenty in preparation for the famine.*

⬆ signet ring   *Draw Pharaoh promoting Joseph using a ring.*

Joseph's Brothers Traveled to Egypt: *The years of famine came, and the whole earth was affected, and Joseph began to open Egypt's storehouses of grain. Joseph's family in Canaan also felt the effects of the extended drought, and his brothers went to Egypt to purchase grain.*

⟡ (2) Canaan, Egypt

©2005   *Draw Joseph's ten brothers on their way to Egypt.*

JOSEPH THE RULER

Bible Verses: Genesis 41:1-50:26
Time Frame: Following Abraham, Isaac, and Jacob

Gen. 41:1-8

2 years later

Pharaoh's Two Dreams

Gen. 41:9-16, 25-36

Gen. 41:37-49

Joseph Before Pharaoh

Joseph, Second in Command

Gen. 41:56-57; 42:1-3

10 Brothers

Egypt →

Joseph's Brothers Traveled to Egypt

SP 56

JOSEPH THE RULER

Joseph and His Brothers Were Reunited: *In the second year of the famine, Joseph's brothers arrived in Egypt to buy grain. After several encounters between Joseph and his brothers, Joseph revealed himself to them. Joseph had forgiven them for selling him into slavery because he saw that God had sent him to Egypt to save his family and others. Joseph requested that his brothers bring his father, Jacob, and their families to Egypt. Pharaoh promised Joseph's family the best of the land of Egypt.*

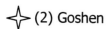 posterity   *Draw Joseph being reunited with his brothers.*

Jacob Moved His Family to Egypt: *God appeared to Jacob and reassured him that he was to move his family to the land of Goshen in Egypt, where God would make his family a great nation. So Jacob moved the whole family to Egypt.*

✦ (2) Goshen

Draw Jacob and his family moving to Egypt.

Joseph Died: *Joseph knew that Egypt was not the land that God had promised Abraham, Isaac, and Jacob. Joseph was confident that the day would come when the children of Israel would return to the Promised Land. When that happened, he wanted to be buried there.*

Draw Joseph's coffin

1. Why was Joseph called before Pharaoh? *To interpret Pharaoh's dreams.*
2. What did Pharaoh dream? *He dreamed about seven thin heads of grain devouring seven plump heads of grain and seven gaunt cows eating seven fat cows.*
3. What did Pharaoh's dreams mean? *There would be seven years of plenty in Egypt followed by seven years of famine.*
4. What was Joseph's new position? *Second in command to Pharaoh.*
5. How old was Joseph when he entered Pharaoh's service? *Thirty.*
6. How did God use Joseph in regard to his family? *God sent Joseph to prepare the way for them to have a secure place to live with plenty of food.*
7. Where did Jacob's family move? *The land of Goshen in Egypt.*
8. What instructions did Joseph leave for the children of Israel regarding his body? *That his body was to be buried in the Promised Land when the children of Israel returned to the land promised by God.*
9. What do we learn about God from these verses? *He knows the end from the beginning, and even when we don't understand why things are happening, we can be assured that they are for our good.*

©2005

86

Gen. 45:1-10, 16-20

Joseph and His Brothers Were Reunited

Gen. 46:1-7, 26-27

Gen. 50:24-26

Joseph
Age 110

Jacob Moved His Family to Egypt

Joseph Died

Lesson Review

1. Why was Joseph called before Pharaoh?
2. What did Pharaoh dream?
3. What did Pharaoh's dreams mean?
4. What was Joseph's new position?
5. How old was Joseph when he entered Pharaoh's service?
6. How did God use Joseph in regard to his family?
7. Where did Jacob's family move?
8. What instructions did Joseph leave for the children of Israel regarding his body?
9. What do we learn about God from these verses?

Memory Verse: Genesis 50:24

SP 57

Review 2

1. What was Job like? *Blameless, upright, feared God, and shunned evil.*

2. How many sons and daughters did Job have altogether? *Fourteen sons and six daughters.*

3. What did Job own altogether? *21,000 sheep, 9,000 camels, 1,500 yoke of oxen, and 1,500 donkeys.*

4. Who appeared before God and tested Job's faith? *Satan.*

5. When Job lost everything, how did he respond? *He grieved but did not sin or accuse God of wrongdoing.*

6. Who came to visit Job? *His three friends, Eliphaz, Bildad, and Zophar.*

7. When God challenged Job, what did God show Job? *That God alone is all-powerful and that Job had an incomplete knowledge of Him.*

8. What did God give Job after his suffering? *More sons and daughters and twice as much wealth as before.*

9. Recite Job 1:22.

10. What did God promise Abram? *To make him a great nation, to give him a great name, to give him a specific land, and that through his family all the families of the earth would be blessed.*

11. Where was Hagar from, and what was her role in the family? *Hagar was from Egypt; she was the maid of Sarai and later Abram's wife.*

12. How did Hagar describe God? *The God Who Sees.*

13. Who was the child promised to Abraham? *Isaac.*

14. How old were Abraham and Sarah when Isaac was born? *Abraham 100/Sarah 90.*

15. What was the promise regarding Ishmael? *His family would grow to be a mighty nation.*

16. What was the promise regarding Isaac? *The promise that God made to Abraham, giving him a specific land, many descendants and that all the nations of the earth would be blessed through his family was continued to Isaac.*

17. Who were Abraham's wives? *Sarah, Hagar, and Keturah.*

18. Recite Genesis 22:18.

SP 58

19. Who were Isaac's father and mother? *Abraham and Sarah.*

20. What did God tell Abraham to do to Isaac? *To sacrifice Isaac.*

21. How did God provide for Abraham in regard to sacrificing Isaac? *God stopped Abraham from sacrificing Isaac and provided a ram in his place.*

22. How did Isaac get a wife? *Abraham sent his servant to find Isaac a wife.*

23. Who was Isaac's wife? *Rebekah.*

24. How old was Isaac when he married? *Forty years old.*

25. Who were Isaac's sons? *Jacob and Esau.*

26. What did God promise Isaac? *The continue the promise that He made to Abraham, giving him a large family, a specific land, and promise that all the nations of the earth would be blessed through his family.*

27. Recite Genesis 26:4.

28. Who were Jacob's father and mother? *Isaac and Rebekah.*

29. Who was Jacob's brother? *Esau.*

30. How did Jacob get the blessing? *By making his father think he was Esau.*

31. Where did Jacob flee, and why did he go? *To Haran because Esau wanted to kill him.*

32. What was Esau's response to Jacob's return? *Esau welcomed Jacob, and there was peace between the brothers.*

33. What did God change Jacob's name to? *Israel.*

34. What did God promise Jacob? *That he would inherit the land promised to Abraham and Isaac and that through his family all the nations of the earth would be blessed.*

35. How many wives did Jacob have? *Four.*

36. How many children did Jacob have? *Thirteen.*

37. Recite Genesis 35:12.

38. Who was Joseph's father? *Jacob/Israel.*

39. What did Joseph's brothers do to him? *They sold him as a slave.*

40. Where was Joseph a slave (country)? *Egypt.*

41. How did Jacob respond to the reports about Joseph being dead? *He mourned greatly.*

42. What was Joseph's job in Potiphar's household? *Overseer.*

43. How did Joseph end up in prison? *Potiphar's wife told a lie about Joseph.*

44. How did God bless Joseph even while he was in prison? *He became overseer of the prison.*

45. Who were the two people that had dreams while in prison with Joseph? *The chief butler and the chief baker.*

46. Recite Genesis 39:2.

47. Why was Joseph called before Pharaoh? *To interpret Pharaoh's dream.*

48. What did Pharaoh dream? *He dreamed about seven thin heads of grain devouring seven plump heads of grain and seven gaunt cows eating seven fat cows.*

49. What did Pharaoh's dream mean? *There would be seven years of plenty in Egypt followed by seven years of famine.*

50. What was Joseph's new position? *Second in command to Pharaoh.*

51. How old was Joseph when he entered Pharaoh's service? *Thirty.*

52. How did God use Joseph in regard to his family? *God sent Joseph to prepare the way for them to have a secure place to live with plenty of food.*

53. Where did Jacob's family move? *The land of Goshen in Egypt.*

54. What instructions did Joseph leave for the children of Israel regarding his body? *That his body was to be buried in the Promised Land when the children of Israel returned to the land promised by God.*

55. Recite Genesis 50:24.

SP 60

Section 4 Goals and Key Points

MOSES

The goal of this lesson is to show that Moses was set apart by God, from birth, to play a special part in God's plan to free the children of Israel from their bondage in Egypt.

Key Points:
- Pharaoh feared the children of Israel because of their vast numbers and strength.
- Moses was born at a time in which all male Hebrew babies, were being killed, and yet his brave parents saved him from death.
- Moses was adopted and lived as the grandson of Pharaoh.
- Moses left Egypt after he killed an Egyptian man who was beating a Hebrew man. (Moses was forty years of age at this time.)
- Moses lived for forty years in Midian, where he married and had two sons.
- God spoke to Moses through a burning bush, and commissioned him to return to Egypt and deliver the children of Egypt out of bondage. (Moses was eighty years of age at this time.)
- Moses returned to Egypt with his family and the rod of God.

THE DELIVERANCE

The goal of this lesson is to teach what God did to show Pharaoh and all those in Egypt that He was indeed God over all the Egyptian gods.

Key Points:
- When Moses returned to Egypt, he went to Pharaoh and asked that the children of Israel be allowed to go and worship. Pharaoh refused this request and laid an even heavier burden on the Israelites.
- God sent ten plagues on Egypt to show Pharaoh and all those in Egypt that He was the most powerful God.
- The first three plagues affected all of Egypt, including Goshen, where the Hebrews lived.
- The last seven plagues affected all of Egypt but not Goshen.

THE EXODUS

The goal of this lesson is to demonstrate how God, with a mighty hand, delivered the children of Israel out of Egypt, under the leadership of Moses.

Key Points:
- The tenth plague was the death of the firstborn.
- After Pharaoh's son died in the last plague, he ordered Moses to take the children of Israel and leave Egypt.
- Those leaving Egypt included the children of Israel and those in Egypt who, having seen the power of God, desired to serve the God of Israel.
- God led the children of Israel with a pillar of cloud by day and a pillar of fire by night.
- God protected the children of Israel when Pharaoh's army pursued them.
- At the Red Sea, God parted the waters, and the children of Israel walked through on dry ground.
- Pharaoh's army drowned as they tried to pursue the children of Israel through the Red Sea.

THE LAW AND THE PROMISES

The goal of this lesson is to explain that God gave us laws to teach us how to live a life pleasing to Him.

Key Points:
- The first four of the Ten Commandments deal with man's relationship to God.
- The last six of the Ten Commandments deal with man's relationship to other men.
- God gave promises associated with our obedience to His law.

THE TABERNACLE

The goal of this lesson is to show that God established a place and system of worship for the children of Israel.

Key Points:
- The central place of worship for the Israelites was the tabernacle.
- The tabernacle was a place of sacrifice and worship and was where God dwelt among His people.
- The tabernacle was built according to the instructions God gave to Moses.
- The furnishings of the tabernacle were built by men who were given skills by God.
- The Levites were in charge of the tabernacle.
- The camp of Israel was set up according to God's instructions and was an orderly camp.

THE TWELVE SPIES

The goal of this lesson is to discover what happened when the Twelve Spies were sent into the Promised Land and returned to give a report to Moses and the children of Israel.

Key Points:
- The Promised Land had fortified cities and strong people, and the land was abundant in what it produced for food.
- Ten of the twelve spies did not want to try to conquer the land that God had promised them and discouraged the children of Israel from going in.
- Two of the twelve spies encouraged the people to trust God and enter the land.
- The children of Israel rebelled against God and as a result were sentenced to forty years in the desert in which all those twenty and over would die, except Joshua and Caleb.
- Although the children of Israel were punished for their sin, God provided for them while they were in the desert.
- While they were in the desert for forty years their clothes and sandals did not wear out, God fed them with manna, and He led them with a pillar of cloud and a pillar of fire.

Level 3

Add to the Joseph card.

- *God promoted Joseph to second in command of all of Egypt.*
- *Joseph married an Egyptian woman and had two sons, Ephraim and Manasseh.*
- *Joseph forgave his brothers for selling him into slavery.*
- *Jacob moved his family from Canaan to Goshen in Egypt.*

Level 4

MOSES

Topical Bible

What was a *Pharaoh*?

> *Nave's, page 365*

Bible Dictionary

What was the *burning bush*?

> *Zondervan's, page 95-96*

Concordance

Give two verses that contain the phrase *land of Egypt*.

> *Genesis 13:10; 41:19, 54 (Cruden's, page 139)*

Quest Question

Does God always hear us when we pray?

> *Yes.*

MOSES

Timeline Review

Jacob   *Jacob's children*   Joseph   *Egypt*

Bible Verses

Genesis 50:24

Genesis 39:2

Genesis 35:12

SP 63

MOSES

Background Bible Reading: Genesis 50-Exodus 4
Time Frame: About 350 years after the Israelites entered Egypt

---

Pharaoh Ordered Death: *Following the death of Joseph and his generation, the new king of Egypt did not remember Joseph or the things that he had done for Egypt. The Pharaoh became afraid of the growing number and strength of the Israelites. Pharaoh ordered the Israelite midwives to kill all the male babies as they were born. However, the midwives feared God rather than Pharaoh. When the midwives did not kill the boys, Pharaoh then commanded his people to throw all the newborn Hebrew boys into the river to die.*

 (2) Egypt, Rameses

midwives, feared God   *Draw Pharaoh ordering "death."*

Moses' Family: *Moses' father was Amram, his mother was Jochebed, his brother was Aaron, and his sister was Miriam. Moses was from the tribe of Levi.*

Draw Amram, Jochebed, Aaron, Miriam, and Moses.

Moses in the Nile River: *Moses' mother hid him for three months, then she made an ark, and covered it with asphalt and pitch. Jochebed then placed baby Moses in the ark and put him in the Nile River under the watchful care of his sister, Miriam.*

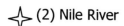 (2) Nile River

ark, asphalt, pitch   *Draw Miriam watching the ark from the bulrushes.*

Moses and the Princess: *As Miriam watched, the ark floated down the Nile River and was drawn out of the water by Pharaoh's daughter. Pharaoh's daughter adopted Moses and raised him as her own son. Jochebed became Moses' nurse and was able to care for Moses until he was weaned.*

Moses   *Draw Pharaoh's daughter at the river holding baby Moses.*

MOSES

Bible Verses: Exodus 1:1-4:20
Time Frame: About 350 years after the Israelites entered Egypt

Ex. 1:1-22

"Death"

Pharaoh Ordered "Death"

Ex. 2:1-2

Amram, Jochebed, Miriam, Aaron

Moses' Family

Ex. 2:3-4

Moses in the Nile River

Ex. 2:5-10

Moses and the Princess

SP 64

MOSES

Moses Left Egypt: *Moses saw a Hebrew being treated badly by an Egyptian, and he killed the Egyptian. Pharaoh found out about the murder and sought to kill Moses. Moses left Egypt and fled to Midian.*

Draw Moses fleeing from Egypt.

Moses in Midian: *Moses fled to Midian (map) where Jethro, the priest of Midian, took him in. Jethro gave Moses his daughter, Zipporah, as his wife and they were blessed with two sons, Gershom and Eliezer. (Ex. 2:22, 18:3-4)*

 (2) Midian

Gershom, Eliezer   *Draw Moses and his family.*

God Heard the Cries of the Israelites: *God heard and remembered His promise to Abraham, Isaac, and Jacob.*

heard, groaning, covenant   *Draw the triangle and the people crying out to God.*

The Burning Bush: *While tending flocks for his father-in-law, Moses saw a bush that was burning but was not consumed. Here we are introduced to God as "I Am." God commissioned Moses to return to Egypt and deliver His people out of bondage.*

holy, I AM   *Draw the burning bush, Moses bowing down, and his sandals set aside.*

Moses Returned to Egypt: *After experiencing God in the burning bush, Moses returned to Egypt with his family and the rod of God.*

Draw Moses returning to Egypt with his family.

---

1. Who wanted to kill the baby boys and why? *Pharaoh, because the children of Israel had grown to be a large and strong people within Egypt.*
2. What did Moses' parents do with baby Moses to protect him from death? They hid him for three months and then made a waterproof ark and put him in the Nile River, with his sister watching.
3. Who found Moses floating in the Nile River? *Pharaoh's daughter.*
4. Why did Moses flee from Egypt? *Because he killed an Egyptian and when Pharaoh found out, he sought to kill Moses.*
5. Where did Moses go when he fled from Egypt? *Midian.*
6. Why did God appear to Moses in the burning bush? *To tell Moses that He had heard the cries of the children of Israel and would deliver them out of bondage.*
7. What do we learn about God from these verses? *God hears us when we cry out to Him and that He is I AM, the one and only God.*

©2005

Ex. 2:11-15

Egypt

Moses Left Egypt

Ex. 2:16-21

Moses in Midian

Ex. 2:23-25

God Heard the Cries of the Israelites

Ex. 3:1-22

Ex. 4:18-20

Egypt

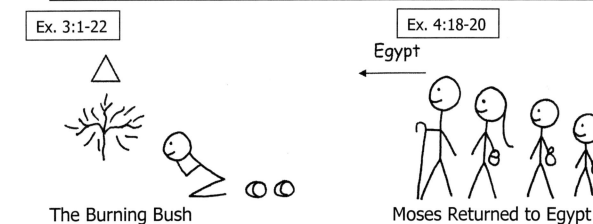

The Burning Bush

Moses Returned to Egypt

Lesson Review

1. Who wanted to kill the baby boys and why?
2. What did Moses' parents do with baby Moses to protect him from death?
3. Who found Moses floating in the Nile River?
4. Why did Moses flee from Egypt?
5. Where did Moses go when he fled from Egypt?
6. Why did God appear to Moses in the burning bush?
7. What do we learn about God from these verses?

Memory Verse: Exodus 2:24

SP 65

Level 3

Create a card for Moses

- *Moses was born to a Levite couple at a time when Pharaoh was trying to kill all Hebrew male infants.*
- *Moses was adopted by the daughter of Pharaoh.*
- *At forty years old, Moses killed an Egyptian and fled from Egypt to Midian.*
- *Moses married Zipporah and had two sons, Gershom and Eliezer.*
- *When Moses was eighty years old God appeared to him in the burning bush commissioning him to return to Egypt and deliver the Hebrews out of bondage.*

Level 4

THE DELIVERANCE

Topical Bible

Give the two countries with which *bondage* is associated in the Bible.

Nave's, page 63

Bible Dictionary

Why were the *plagues of Egypt* sent by God?

Zondervan's, page 462

Concordance

How many times in the Bible did God state *"I am the Lord"*?

Cruden's, page 299

Quest Question

Compare the God of the Bible to other gods.

Answers will vary.

SP 66

THE DELIVERANCE

Timeline Review

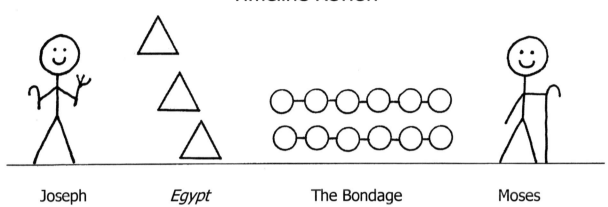

| Joseph | *Egypt* | The Bondage | Moses |

Bible Verses

Exodus 2:24

Genesis 50:24

Genesis 39:2

SP 67

THE DELIVERANCE

Background Bible Reading: Exodus 1-10
Time Frame: 430 years after the Israelites entered Egypt (Gen. 15:13, Ex. 12:40)

The Request: *In obedience to the call of God, Moses and Aaron went before Pharaoh to request that the children of Israel be allowed to take a three-day journey into the wilderness to sacrifice and worship God.*

Draw Moses and Aaron before Pharaoh.

The Punishment: *Pharaoh was upset at the request, and instead of granting it he increased the work load of all the Israelites in Egypt.*

Draw a man making bricks and another running with straw.

The Plagues: *God sent the plagues because Pharaoh hardened his heart toward God and would not let the children of Israel go to worship Him. Beginning with the 4th plague, God differentiates between His people in Goshen and Pharaoh's people throughout Egypt (Ex. 8:22-23). God sent the plagues to show Pharaoh, his officials, and all in Egypt that there was only one true God, the God of the Israelites.*

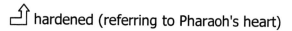 hardened (referring to Pharaoh's heart)

Individual study of the plagues is recommended. One purpose of the plagues was to show that the God of Abraham, Isaac, and Jacob was the one and only God. The references beside the plagues are given to show this concept.

Water Became blood: *Exodus 7:17 "By this you shall know that I am the Lord."*

Draw red water.

Frogs: *Exodus 8:10 "...that you may know that there is no one like the Lord our God."*

Draw frogs.

Lice: *Exodus 8:19 "...This is the finger of God."*

Draw lice.

Flies: *Exodus 8:22 "...that you may know that I am the Lord in the midst of the land."*

Draw people with flies and label "Egypt"/ people without flies and label "Goshen."

THE DELIVERANCE

Bible Verses: Exodus 5:1-10:2
Time Frame: 430 years after the children of Israel entered Egypt

| Ex. 5:1-4 | Ex. 5:5-8 |

Moses   Aaron

The Request   The Punishment

The Plagues

Ex. 7:14-16

Ex. 7:17-21   1. Water became blood

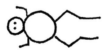
Ex. 8:5-6   2. Frogs
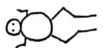

Ex. 8:16-17   3. Lice

Ex. 8:20-23   4. Flies

Egypt   Goshen

SP 68

THE DELIVERANCE

Dead livestock: *Exodus 9:1-6*

Draw dead livestock.

Boils: *Exodus 9:10-11*

Draw boils on a man and an animal.

Hail: *Exodus 9:14 "...that you may know that there is none like Me in all the earth."*
Exodus 9:29 "...that you may know that the earth is the Lord's."

Draw a man running and large hail falling.

Locusts: *Exodus 10:2 "that you may know that I am the Lord."*

Draw locust on wheat.

Darkness: *Exodus 10:22-23*

Draw darkness.

Reasons for the Plagues: (1) *To show that the God of Israel is the one and only God and more powerful than Egyptian gods.* (2) *For the Israelites to see God's deliverance and then tell their children about what God had done.* (3) *For the people of Egypt to have an opportunity to worship and serve the God of Abraham, Isaac, and Jacob.*

Note reasons for plagues.

---

1. Why did Moses and Aaron go to Pharaoh? *To request that the children of Israel be allowed to take a 3-day journey into the wilderness to sacrifice and worship God.*
2. What was Pharaoh's response to Moses' request? *Pharaoh increased the workload of the Israelites in bondage, demanding that they find their own straw with which to make the bricks while producing the same number as before.*
3. Name the first nine plagues? *1. water to blood 2. frogs   3. lice   4. flies   5. dead livestock   6. boils 7. hail 8. locust 9. darkness.*
4. Why were the plagues sent? *To show all those in Egypt who the one and only true God was and that He was more powerful than all their Egyptian gods.*
5. Who did the plagues affect? *Plagues 1-3 struck those in both Egypt and Goshen; plagues 4-9 struck only those in Egypt.*
6. What do we learn about God from these verses? *God is over every god that man can worship; He is the only true God.*

Ex. 9:1-6	5. Dead Livestock
Ex. 9:10-11	6. Boils
Ex. 9:18-26	7. Hail
Ex. 10:13-15	8. Locust
Ex. 10:22-23	9. Darkness

Reasons for the Plagues

| Ex. 8:10; 9:29 | 1. *To show that the God of Israel is the one and only God and more powerful than Egyptian gods.* |

| Ex. 10:1-2 | 2. *For the Israelites to see God's deliverance and then tell their children about what God had done.* |

| Ex. 12:38 | 3. *For the people of Egypt to have an opportunity to worship and serve the God of Abraham, Isaac, and Jacob.* |

Lesson Review

1. Why did Moses and Aaron go to Pharaoh?
2. What was Pharaoh's response to Moses' request?
3. Name the first nine plagues.
4. Why were the plagues sent?
5. Who did the plagues affect?
6. What do we learn about God from these verses?

Memory Verse: Exodus 10:2

SP 69

Level 3

Create a card for the Ten Plagues.

1. *Water to blood.*
2. *Frogs.*
3. *Lice.*
4. *Flies.*
5. *Dead livestock.*
6. *Boils.*
7. *Hail.*
8. *Locusts.*
9. *Darkness.*

Level 4

THE EXODUS

Topical Bible

If you were researching the *Passover,* what verses would you begin with?

Exodus 12:3-49 (Nave's, page 354)

Bible Dictionary

What does *Exodus* mean?

Zondervan's, page 163

Concordance

What is the first reference to the *Red Sea* ?

Exodus 10:19 (Cruden's, page 396)

Quest Question

Does God kill people?

Yes, but remember that God is always just and fair in His dealing with all men.

THE EXODUS

Timeline Review

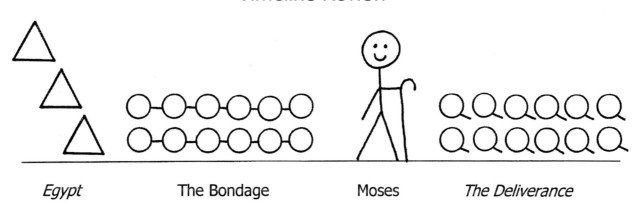

Egypt　　　The Bondage　　　Moses　　　*The Deliverance*

Bible Verses

Exodus 10:2

Exodus 2:24

Genesis 50:24

SP 71

THE EXODUS

Background Bible Reading: Exodus 10-14
Time Frame: 430 years after the Israelites entered Egypt

The Lamb: *The lamb/goat eaten at the first Passover meal was to be without blemish, a male, a year old. Each household (or combined households) were to choose the lamb on the tenth day of the first month and kill it on the fourteenth day at twilight.*

 blemish   *Draw a lamb and note: one year, without blemish, and male.*

The Doorposts: *The blood of the lamb/goat was then put on the lintel and doorposts of the homes.*

 lintel   *Draw blood over a door.*

The Meal: *The Passover meal consisted of roasted lamb/goat (not raw or boiled), unleavened bread, and bitter herbs.*

 bitter herbs, unleavened   *Draw a table and label lamb, unleavened bread, and bitter herbs.*

Death of the Firstborn: *The tenth plague on Egypt would kill every firstborn man and animal whose home was not protected by the blood of the lamb/goat. It was on the night of the first Passover that all of the firstborn of Egypt died, including the firstborn son of Pharaoh.*

 firstborn   *Draw Pharaoh at his son's bed.*

Pharaoh's Command: *Following the death of his son, Pharaoh commanded the children of Israel to leave Egypt.*

Draw Pharaoh issuing a command

THE EXODUS

Bible Verses: Exodus 11:9-14:31

Time Frame: 430 years after the children of Israel entered Egypt

Ex. 11:9-10; 12:1, 5-8

1 year old
Without blemish
Male

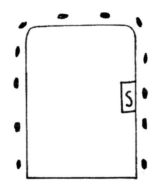

| The Lamb | The Doorposts | The Meal |

Ex. 12:12-13, 29-32

The Tenth Plague

"OUT!"

Death of the Firstborn   Pharaoh's Command

SP 72

THE EXODUS

The Exodus: *The children of Israel plundered the Egyptians when the Lord delivered 600,000 men, plus women and children, out of Egypt. The children of Israel also took the coffin of Joseph with them (Gen. 50:24-26). God led Israel into the desert with a pillar of cloud by day and a pillar of fire by night.*

 (2) Rameses, Succoth

 plunder, mixed multitude   *Draw people leaving behind a cloud and a camp.*

Pharaoh Changed His Mind: *Upon realizing what he had done, Pharaoh changed his mind and pursued the children of Israel with 600 chariots and his army.*

Draw Pharaoh in a chariot.

The Red Sea: *When the children of Israel saw Pharaoh and his army approaching they cried out to God and Moses. God told Moses to lift up his rod and stretch it over the sea; then the Lord sent a wind and the sea parted.*

 (2) Red Sea   *Draw Moses walking through the parted sea.*

God Protected His People: *When Pharaoh's army drew near, the Lord prevented the army from attacking the Israelites by putting the Angel of the Lord and the pillar of cloud/fire between the two camps.*

Draw Pharaoh's army on one side of the pillar of cloud and the camp of Israel on the other.

Pharaoh's Army: *Pharaoh's army pursued the Israelites into the Red Sea. Once the Israelites had crossed, God told Moses to stretch out his hand, and when he did, the sea returned to its normal depth, killing all of Pharaoh's army.*

Draw Pharaoh's dead army in the Red Sea.

1. What were the children of Israel commanded to do on the night of the Passover? *Kill a lamb/goat and eat it with bitter herbs and unleavened bread, then take the lamb/goat's blood and put it over the lintels and doorposts.*
2. Whom did the tenth plague affect? *Every firstborn man and animal that did not have the blood on their doorposts, including Pharaoh's own son.*
3. Following the tenth plague, what did Pharaoh do? *He let the children of Israel go.*
4. Who left Egypt and with what did they leave? *600,000 men, plus women and children, along with their animals and what they plundered from the Egyptians.*
5. How were the children of Israel led once they left Egypt? *God led them with a pillar of cloud by day and a pillar of fire by night.*
6. What did Pharaoh do after the children of Israel had left? *Changed his mind and went after them.*
7. What happened at the Red Sea? *God parted the sea, the children of Israel went through on dry ground, and Pharaoh's army was drowned.*
8. What do we learn about God from these verses? God *takes care of us when we are obedient to Him.*

©2005

110

Ex. 12:35-38; 13:18-22

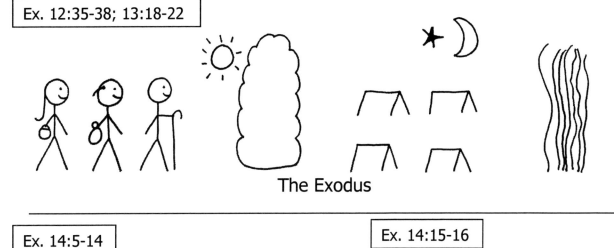

The Exodus

Ex. 14:5-14

Pharaoh Changed His Mind

Ex. 14:15-16

The Red Sea

Ex. 14:19-20

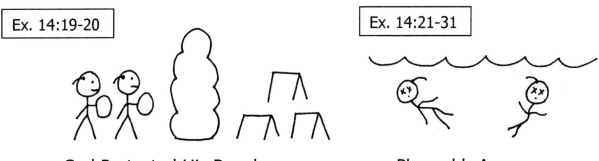

God Protected His People

Ex. 14:21-31

Pharaoh's Army

Lesson Review

1. What were the children of Israel commanded to do on the night of the Passover?
2. Whom did the tenth plague affect?
3. Following the tenth plague, what did Pharaoh do?
4. Who left Egypt and with what did they leave?
5. How were the children of Israel led once they left Egypt?
6. What did Pharaoh do after the children of Israel had left?
7. What happened at the Red Sea?
8. What do we learn about God from these verses?

Memory Verse: Exodus 15:19

SP 73

Level 3

Add to the Ten Plagues card.

> *10. The death of the firstborn.*

Create a card for The Exodus.

- *The Exodus out of Egypt took place after God sent the tenth plague on Egypt.*
- *Pharaoh commanded the children of Israel to leave Egypt after his son died in the last plague.*
- *God led and protected the Israelites with a pillar of cloud and a pillar of fire.*
- *God parted to Red Sea to allow the Israelites to escape Pharaoh's army.*
- *Pharaoh's army drowned in the Red Sea when they tried to pursue the Israelites.*

Level 4

THE LAW AND THE PROMISES

Topical Bible

What other English words can be used to mean *commandment*?

> *Nave's, page 89*

Bible Dictionary

What is the first definition of the l*aw*?

> *Zondervan's, page 319*

Concordance

Give the Biblical reference for this verse: "Now therefore if you will indeed *obey* My voice and keep My covenant, then you shall be a special treasure...."

> *Exodus 19:5. (Cruden's, page 342)*

Quest Question

Should we, as God's people, still obey the Ten Commandments?

> *Yes.*

SP 74

THE LAW AND THE PROMISES

Timeline Review

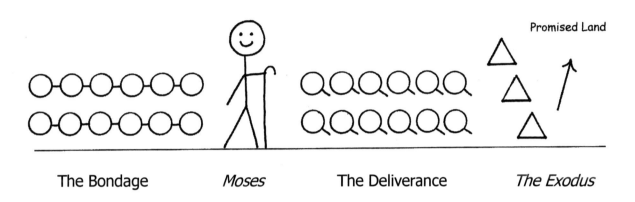

The Bondage   *Moses*   The Deliverance   *The Exodus*

Bible Verses

Exodus 15:19

Exodus 10:2

Exodus 2:24

THE LAW AND THE PROMISES

Background Bible Reading: Exodus 15-24
Time Frame: After the Exodus, while they were in the desert

Moses at Mount Sinai: *Three months after leaving Egypt, the children of Israel arrived at Mount Sinai. God reminded them of their deliverance out of Egypt and began to outline His expectations of them. Here we begin to see the IF/THEN passages of the Bible. If the people obeyed God's commands, then God promised them they would be His special people, a holy nation, and a kingdom of priests.*

Draw God, Moses and two tablets.

The Ten Commandments: *I recommend a word study on each of the commandments. The Ten Commandments are written using the New King James Version.*

1. Unlike any other nation, Israel was to worship only one God.

⬆ gods, before   *Draw a purple triangle.*

---

2. Unlike other forms of worship, God would not let Himself be represented by any graven image.

⬆ graven image   *Draw a graven image and a circle around it with a line through it.*

---

3. God wants us to seriously consider how we use His name. "Take" can be translated "carry". God is concerned not only with our words, but also how we carry His name.

⬆ take, vain   *Draw a man with little triangles coming out of his mouth.*

---

4. For six 6 days we are to work, and then we are to take a Sabbath to the Lord.

⬆ Sabbath, holy, work   *Draw a calendar.*

---

5. The only commandment with a promise.

⬆ honor, days, long, well   *Draw your Dad and Mom.*

©2005

114

THE LAW AND THE PROMISES

Bible Verses: Exodus 19:1-24:31
Time Frame: After the Exodus, while they were in the desert

| Ex. 19:1-8 | Mount Sinai | 3 months later |

  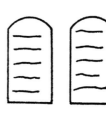

Moses at Mount Sinai

The Ten Commandments

Laws Regarding Man's Relationship to God

| Ex. 20:1-3 | 1. You shall have no other gods before Me. | |

| Ex. 20:4-6 | 2. You shall not make any graven images. | |

| Ex. 20:7 | 3. You shall not take the name of the Lord your God in vain. |

| Ex. 20:8-11 | 4. You shall remember the Sabbath and keep it holy. |

1, 2, 3, 4, 5, 6 △

Laws regarding man's relationship to man

| Ex. 20:12 | 5. Honor your father and your mother... | |

SP 76

THE LAW AND THE PROMISES

6. Murder and kill are not the same and must be distinguished here.

⌂ murder   *Draw a man killing another man.*

7. Unlike some religions or practices, God requires faithfulness in marriage.

⌂ adultery   *Draw a man and woman kissing.*

8. God has promised to supply what we need.

⌂ steal   *Draw a man holding something behind his back.*

9. There are many verses on lying and the tongue.

⌂ false witness   *Draw a judge and a witness.*

10. God wants us to be content with what He has given us.

⌂ covet   *Draw a man with a little car looking at a bigger car.*

The Promises:

1. *If they were obedient, they would be set apart to Him.*

2. *If they were obedient, they would be a holy people, set apart from other people.*

3. *If they were obedient, they would dwell long in the land of promise.*

4. *If they were obedient, they would be set above other nations.*

⌂ set apart, holy, obedient

1. How did God give the laws and promises to the children of Israel? *God spoke to Moses, who then told the people.*
2. The first four commandments concern man's relationship with whom? *God.*
3. The last six commandments concern man's relationship with whom? *Other men.*
4. Why did God give them the laws? *To make them a separate people set apart to God.*
5. What did God promise to the children of Israel? *That they would be a special and holy people unto Him. If they were obedient to His laws, they would live long in the land of promise and be over other nations.*
6. What do we learn about God from these verses? *God is holy and wants us to be holy. God has standards by which we are to live to please Him. With these standards come promises and blessings when we are obedient.*

Ex. 20:13

6. You shall not murder.

Ex. 20:14

7. You shall not commit adultery.

Ex. 20:15

8. You shall not steal.

Ex. 20:16

9. You shall not bear false witness against your neighbor.

Ex. 20:17

10. You shall not covet.

If the people obeyed God's laws, then they would:

Ex. 19:4-6

1. *Be set apart to God.*

Lev. 20:26

2. *Be holy and separate from other people.*

Deut. 5:32-33

3. *Live long in the land of promise.*

Deut. 28:1

4. *Be set above other nations.*

Lesson Review

1. How did God give the laws and promises to the children of Israel?
2. The first four commandments concern man's relationship to whom?
3. The last six commandments concern man's relationship to whom?
4. Why did God give them the laws?
5. What did God promise to the children of Israel?
6. What do we learn about God from these verses?

Memory Verse: Deuteronomy 6:5

SP 77

Level 3

Create a card for the Ten Commandments.

1. You shall have no other gods before me.

2. You shall not make any graven images.

3. You shall not take the name of the Lord your God in vain.

4. You shall remember the Sabbath and keep it holy.

5. You shall honor your father and mother.

6. You shall not murder.

7. You shall not commit adultery.

8. You shall not steal.

9. You shall not bear false witness against your neighbor.

10. You shall not covet.

Level 4

THE TABERNACLE

Topical Bible

If you were researching the furniture of the *tabernacle*, what would be the first set of verses you would look up?

> *Exodus 25:10-40 (Nave's, page 471)*

Bible Dictionary

What is the first definition of the *tabernacle* ?

> *Zondervan's, page 574*

Concordance

How many times is the tribe of *Levi* referred to in the Bible?

> *18 times (Cruden's, page 288)*

Quest Question

What or where is place of worship for God's people today?

> *Answers will vary.*

©2005

SP 78

THE TABERNACLE

Timeline Review

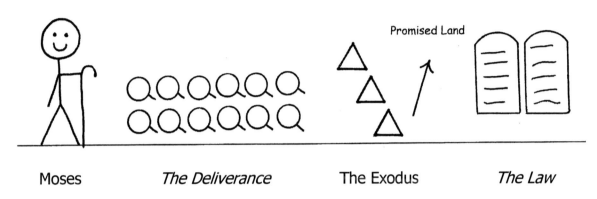

Moses   *The Deliverance*   The Exodus   *The Law*

Bible Verses

Deuteronomy 6:5

Exodus 15:19

Exodus 10:2

SP 79

THE TABERNACLE

Background Bible Reading: Exodus 24-37, Numbers 1-2
Time Frame: After the Exodus, while in the desert

The Lord Gave Moses Instructions: *God called Moses to Mount Sinai, and for forty days He gave him instructions concerning the building and furnishings of the tabernacle. Later Moses received instructions concerning the priests and Levites who served in the tabernacle and the craftsmen who built it.*

Draw God and Moses.

The Tabernacle: *The frame of the tabernacle was made of wood, overlaid with gold with a tent-like covering. The tabernacle was divided into two sections, the Holy of Holies and the Holy Place. A courtyard surrounded the tabernacle, and a curtain separated this courtyard from the camp of Israel. The tabernacle was a place of worship and sacrifice.*

 cubit

The Ark of the Covenant: *The ark was made of wood and overlaid with gold. The lid had two cherubim on it and was called the mercy seat, because here God spoke to His people. The ark was located in the Holy of Holies.*

Draw the ark.

The Table of Showbread: *This table was a wooden table overlaid with gold. The table held the "showbread," 12 loaves of bread that were always before the Lord. The table was located in the Holy Place.*

Draw the Table with two loaves of showbread.

The Golden Lampstand: *The lampstand was a seven-branched lamp made of one piece of gold. The lampstand was located in the Holy Place across from the table of showbread.*

Draw the lampstand.

The Altar of Incense: *The altar of incense was a square box overlaid with gold in which incense was offered to the Lord. The altar was located in the Holy Place, in front of the veil that separated the Holy Place from the Holy of Holies.*

Draw the altar.

The Bronze Laver: *The laver was a basin made of bronze that was located in the courtyard between the Holy Place and the altar of burnt offerings. The priests used the laver to wash their hands and feet before serving in the tabernacle.*

Draw the laver.

The Altar of Burnt Offerings: *The Altar of Burnt Offerings was made of wood and covered in bronze. It was located in the Courtyard. Here the priests offered the burnt offerings from the children of Israel to God.*

Draw the altar in the courtyard.

The Tabernacle

Bible Verses: Exodus 24-31; Numbers 1-2
Time Frame: After the Exodus, while in the desert

Ex. 24:18; 25:1, 8-9

The Lord Gave Moses Instructions

The Tabernacle

A Place of Worship and Sacrifice

Ex. 25:10-11, 21-22	The Ark of the Covenant
Ex. 25:23, 24, 30	The Table of Showbread
Ex. 25:31-32	The Gold Lampstand
Ex. 30:1-3	The Altar of Incense
Ex. 30:18-20	The Bronze Laver
Ex. 27:1-2	The Altar of Burnt Offerings
Ex. 31:1-6	The Craftsmen
Num. 1:50-51; 3:6-8	The Levites

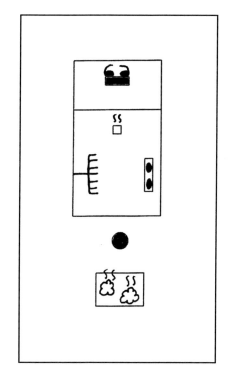

SP 80

THE TABERNACLE

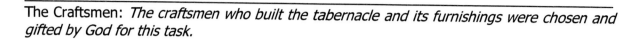

The Craftsmen: *The craftsmen who built the tabernacle and its furnishings were chosen and gifted by God for this task.*

The Levites: *The Levites were chosen by God to be the priests who served Him in the tabernacle. They were also in charge of caring for, moving, and setting up the tabernacle and the articles of the tabernacle.*

The Camp of Israel: *God prescribed an orderly assembly, with each tribe camping under its own banner. The tribe of Levi was assigned to camp around the tabernacle. When labeling each tribe, add up the number of people for each direction. What becomes apparent in the shape of the camp?*

 banner   *Write in each tribe and then draw the cross around the camp.*

(*Teachers will need decide which verses they want their students to read regarding the camp set-up. No review for this lesson is given.)

Num. 1:52-53

Num. 2:1-34

The Camp of Israel

West
*Ephraim
Manasseh
Benjamin
108,100*

South
*Reuben
Simeon
Gad
151,450*

North
*Dan
Asher
Naphtali
157,600*

East
*Judah
Issachar
Zebulun
186,400*

Memory Verse: Exodus 29:45

SP 81

©2005

Level 3

Create a card for The Tabernacle.

- *God gave Moses the plans to build the tabernacle and skilled men to do the work on the Tabernacle.*
- *The tabernacle was a place of worship and sacrifice and a place where God dwelt among His people.*
- *The tabernacle was divided in to three parts: the outer court, the Holy Place, and the Most Holy Place.*
- *The tabernacle was set up in the center of the camp of Israel.*
- *The tribe of Levi was assigned to take care of the tabernacle and its furnishings.*

Level 4

THE TWELVE SPIES

Topical Bible

What were the twelve *spies* sent to do?

> *Nave's, page 461*

Bible Dictionary

What was a fortified city (look up *fort, fortress*)?

> *Zondervan's, page 180*

Concordance

What is the first reference to the man *Caleb* in the Bible?

> *Numbers 13:6 (Cruden's, page 55)*

Quest Question

When we ask God to forgive us of our sins, does that eliminate the consequences of our sins?

> *No; see today's lesson.*

SP 82

THE TWELVE SPIES

Timeline Review

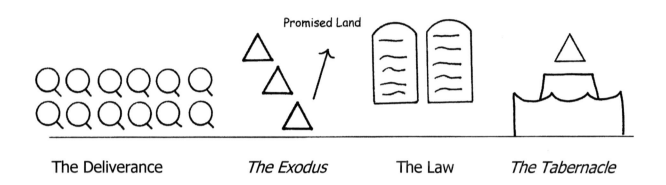

| The Deliverance | *The Exodus* | The Law | *The Tabernacle* |

Bible Verses

Exodus 29:45

Deuteronomy 6:5

Exodus 15:19

SP 83

THE TWELVE SPIES

Background Bible Reading: Numbers 13-14; Deuteronomy 8-9
Time Frame: About six months after leaving Egypt

The Mission: *God instructed Moses to choose twelve men, one from each tribe, to go and spy out the land He was giving them, known as Canaan. They were commissioned to find out what the land, the people, and the cities were like.*

Draw Moses giving the twelve spies instructions.

The Land: *After forty days the spies returned to tell of a land that truly flowed with milk and honey. The spies brought back one cluster of grapes so large that it took two men to carry it. The land was very good.*

Draw milk, honey, and fruit.

The People: *The people of the land were strong and some were descendants of Anak, the giants.*

Draw a strong man and a giant.

The Cities: *The cities were strong, fortified, and very large.*

Anak, fortified   *Draw a fortified city.*

The Decision: *Caleb encouraged the people to go in and conquer the land. Joshua exhorted the people not to be afraid and not to rebel against God because God had promised to be with them. However, the remaining ten spies discouraged the people from trying to conquer the land, saying that the Israelites were not strong enough. The people listened to the ten spies, then cried out in rebellion against Moses and Aaron and attempted to stone them. At that moment the glory of the Lord appeared over the tabernacle and stopped the people from killing them.*

Draw ten spies pointing one direction, two spies pointing the other direction, and Moses praying.

THE TWELVE SPIES

Bible Verses: Numbers 13:1-14:38
Time Frame: About six months after leaving Egypt

Num. 13:1-3, 17-20

12 Spies

The Mission

Num. 13:21-28

Milk
Honey
Fruit

The Land

Strong   Giants

The People

Fortified

The Cities

Num. 13:30

The Decision

Num. 13:31-33; 14:1-10

Joshua

Caleb

SP 84

THE TWELVE SPIES

The Consequences: *God was very angry with the children of Israel's rebellion against His instructions. Although the people tried to stone Moses, he interceded for them. God chose not to destroy them but punished them for their sin of rebellion. The children of Israel would wander in the desert one year for every day that the spies were in the land—forty years. Everyone, except for Joshua and Caleb, who was twenty years or older would die and not see the Promised Land.*

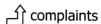 complaints   *Draw graves and wandering dots.*

The Forty Years in the Desert: *Although the children of Israel were under the penalty for their sin, God provided for them in the desert: manna for food, clothes and sandals that did not wear out, and the cloud of His presence to lead them as they traveled.*

 test   *Draw a pillar of cloud, manna, and sandals/clothes.*

1. How many spies were sent to spy out the Promised Land? *Twelve, one from each tribe of Israel.*
2. What were the spies sent to find out? *What the land, people, and cities were like.*
3. How long were the spies in the Promised Land? *Forty days.*
4. Describe the land, the people, and the cities that the spies found. *Land: full of milk, honey, and fruit. People: strong and some giants. Cities: strong, fortified, and very large.*
5. What decision did the children of Israel make? *They decided not to follow God's instructions to go into the Promised Land and attempted to stone Moses.*
6. What were the consequences of their decision? *All those over the age of twenty would die, except Joshua and Caleb, and they would wander in the desert for forty years.*
7. How did God provide for the children of Israel for the forty years in the wilderness? *God led them in the desert, provided them with daily food, manna, and their clothes and sandals did not wear out.*
8. What do we learn about God from these verses? *God will test our hearts to see if we will follow Him.*

©2005

Num. 14:26-30

Num. 14:31-38

20 years and older died

40 years in the desert

The Consequences

___

Deut. 8:2-4; 29:5

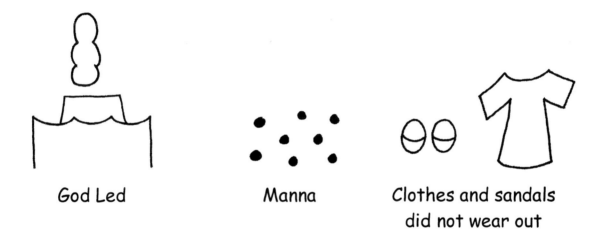

God Led   Manna   Clothes and sandals
                                 did not wear out

Forty Years in the Desert

___

Lesson Review

1. How many spies were sent to spy out the Promised Land?
2. What were the spies sent to find out?
3. How long were the spies in the Promised Land?
4. Describe the land, the people, and the cities that the spies found.
5. What decision did the children of Israel make?
6. What were the consequences of their decision?
7. How did God provide for the children of Israel for the forty years in the wilderness?
8. What do we learn about God from these verses?

Memory Verse: Deuteronomy 8:2

SP 85

Review 3

1. Who wanted to kill the Hebrew baby boys born in Egypt and why? *Pharaoh, because the children of Israel had grown to be a large and strong people within Egypt.*

2. What did Moses' parents do with baby Moses to protect him from death? *They hid him for three months and then made a waterproof ark and put him in the Nile River, with his sister watching.*

3. Who found Moses floating in the Nile River? *Pharaoh's daughter.*

4. Why did Moses flee from Egypt? *Because he killed an Egyptian, and when Pharaoh found out, he sought to kill Moses.*

5. Where did Moses go when he fled from Egypt? *Midian.*

6. Why did God appear to Moses in the burning bush? *To tell Moses that He had heard the cries of the children of Israel and would deliver them out of bondage.*

7. Recite Exodus 2:24.

8. Why did Moses and Aaron go to Pharaoh? *To request that the children of Israel be allowed to take a three-day journey into the wilderness to sacrifice and worship God.*

9. What was Pharaoh's response to Moses' request? *Pharaoh increased the workload of the Israelites in bondage, demanding that they find their own straw with which to make the bricks while producing the same number as before.*

10. Name the first nine plagues. *1. water to blood 2. frogs 3. lice 4. flies 5. dead livestock 6. boils 7. hail 8. locust 9. darkness.*

11. Why were the plagues sent? *To show all those in Egypt who was the one and only true God was and that He was more powerful than all their Egyptian gods.*

12. Who did the plagues affect? *Plagues 1-3 struck those in both Egypt and Goshen; plagues 4-9 struck only Egypt.*

13. Recite Exodus 10:2.

14. What were the children of Israel commanded to do on the night of the Passover? *Kill a lamb/goat and eat it with bitter herbs and unleavened bread, then take the lamb/goat's blood and put it over the lintels and doorposts.*

15. Whom did the tenth plague affect? *Every firstborn man and animal that did not have the blood on their doorposts, including Pharaoh's own son.*

16. Following the tenth plague, what did Pharaoh do? *He let the children of Israel go.*

17. Who left Egypt and with what did they leave? *600,000 men, plus women and children, their animals and what they plundered from the Egyptians.*

SP 86

18. How were the children of Israel lead once they left Egypt? *A pillar of cloud by day and a pillar of fire by night.*

19. What did Pharaoh do after the children of Israel left? *He changed his mind and went after the children of Israel.*

20. What happened at the Red Sea? *God parted the sea, the children of Israel went through on dry ground and Pharaoh's army was drowned.*

21. Recite Exodus 15:19.

22. How did God give the laws and promises to the children of Israel? *God spoke to Moses, who then told the people.*

23. The first four commandments concern man's relationship with whom? *God.*

24. The last six commandments concern man' relationship to whom? *Other men.*

25. Why did God give them the laws? *To make them a separate and set apart people to God.*

26. What did God promise to the children of Israel? *That they would be a special and holy people unto Him. If they were obedient to His laws they would live long in the land of promise and be over other nations.*

27. Recite Deuteronomy 6:5.

28. What was the purpose for the tabernacle? *It was a place of worship and sacrifice for the people and a place where God dwelt among His people.*

29. Recite Exodus 29:45.

30. How many spies were sent to spy out the Promised Land? *Twelve, one from each tribe of Israel.*

31. What were the spies sent to find out? *The state of the land, the people, and the cities.*

32. How long were the spies in the Promised Land? *Forty days.*

33. Describe the land, the people, and the cities that the spies found? *Land: full of milk, honey, and fruit. People: strong and some giants. Cities: strong, fortified, and very large.*

34. What decision did the children of Israel make? *They decided not to follow God's instructions to go into the Promised Land and attempted to stone Moses.*

35. What were the consequences of their decision? *All those over the age of twenty would die, except Joshua and Caleb, and they would wander in the desert for forty years.*

36. How did God provide for the children of Israel for the forty years in the wilderness? *God led them in the desert, provided them with daily food, manna, and their clothes and sandals did not wear out.*

37. Recite Deuteronomy 8:2.

Mid~Series Review

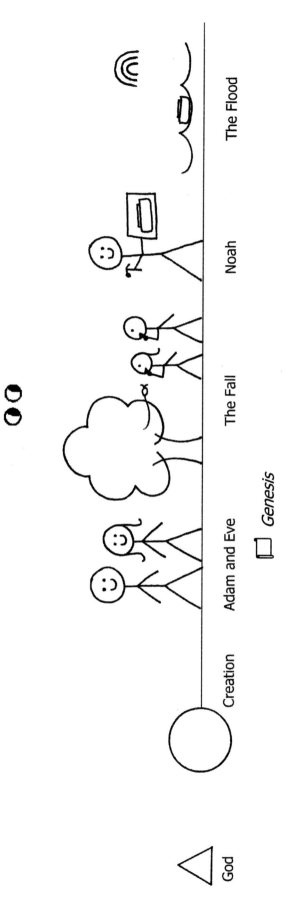

| God | Creation | Adam and Eve | The Fall | Noah | The Flood |

📖 *Genesis*

Recite or write out the following verses on a separate sheet of paper.

1. Genesis 1:1

2. Genesis 1:31

3. Genesis 2:7

4. Genesis 3:15

5. Genesis 6:8

Old Testament Timeline

The Tower   Job   Abraham   Isaac   Jacob

Genesis   Job   Genesis

6. Genesis 11:9

7. Job 1:22

8. Genesis 22:18

9. Genesis 26:4

10. Genesis 35:12

Old Testament Timeline

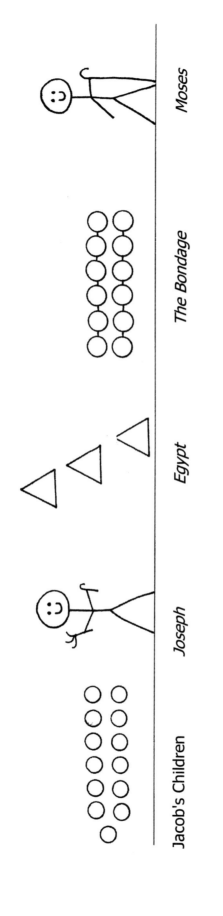

Jacob's Children Joseph Egypt The Bondage Moses

☐ Genesis   ☐ Exodus

11. Jacob had *12* sons and *1* daughter.

12. Genesis 39:2

13. Genesis 50:24

14. The children of Israel were in Egypt for *430* years.

15. Exodus 2:24

Old Testament Timeline

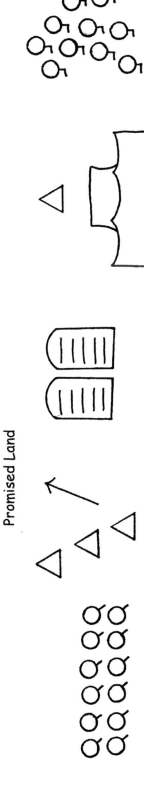

Promised Land

| The Deliverance | The Exodus | The Law | The Tabernacle | The Twelve Spies |

☐ Exodus

☐ Leviticus, Numbers, Deuteronomy

16. Exodus 10:2

17. Exodus 15:19

18. Deuteronomy 6:5

19. Exodus 29:45

20. Deuteronomy 8:2

Section 5 Goals and Key Points

THE PROMISED LAND

The goal of this lesson is to establish the instructions and warnings that God gave the children of Israel before they entered the Promised Land.

Key Points:
- The land promised to Abraham, Isaac, and Jacob was called Canaan at the time of Moses.
- God removed the people of the land (the Canaanites) because of their great wickedness.
- God gave the children of Israel three instructions for when they entered the land:
  1. They were to make no covenants with the people of the land.
  2. They were to completely remove all the people living in the land.
  3. They were to completely destroy all the altars, high places, and idols used to worship other gods.
- God gave the children of Israel two warnings about what would happen if they failed to follow through on His instruction:
  1. Any people left in the land would be a constant source of irritation to the Israelites.
  2. Any people and/or high places left in the land would lure the Israelites into idolatry.
- The Promised Land would be divided among the tribes of Israel according to lot and the size of each tribe.
- The Levites would not have a specific land but instead would have cities throughout the land.

JORDAN AND JERICHO

The goal of this lesson is to show how God established Joshua as leader of the children of Israel as they entered and began the conquest of the Promised Land.

Key Points:
- Before Moses died, God allowed him to see the Promised Land from Mount Nebo.
- After the death of Moses, God appointed Joshua as the leader of the children of Israel.
- Before crossing the Jordan River, Joshua sent two spies into Jericho.
- God stopped the floodwaters of the Jordan River, and the children of Israel walked across the Jordan on dry ground.
- God instructed Joshua to have the army, the priests, and the Levites march quietly around the city one time each day for six days.
- God told Joshua that on the seventh day the army, the priests, and the Levites were to march around the city seven times and then give a shout.
- When the Israelites shouted on the seventh day, the walls of Jericho fell down flat; the city was defeated.

THE JUDGES

The goal of this lesson is to examine what the time of the judges of Israel was like.

Key Points:
- The time of the judges started after the death of Joshua and the elders who served with him. The time of the judges was approximately 400 years; the last judge was Samuel.
- The time of the judges followed the cycle of: rebel, bondage, repentance, judge.
- One of the judges of Israel was Gideon.
- God defeated the armies of the Midianite and Amalekite armies with Gideon and his army of 300 men.
- The time of the judges can be summed up with the last verse of the book: "In those days there was no king in Israel and each man did what was right in his own eyes." (Judges 21:25)

RUTH

The goal of this lesson is to show that like Ruth, people of any nation can choose to serve the God of Abraham, Isaac, and Jacob and become part of God's people.

Key Points:
- Naomi and her husband moved to Moab when there was a famine in Israel.
- Naomi's husband died in Moab; her sons married Moabite women and died while young.
- Ruth, one of Naomi's two daughters-in-law, decided to return to Israel with Naomi.
- Once back in Israel, Ruth married a man named Boaz.
- Boaz and Ruth had a son named Obed.

SAMUEL

The goal of this lesson is to show that Samuel was a man who served God from childhood.

Key Points:
- Hannah prayed for a son, and God gave her Samuel.
- Samuel went to serve God in Shiloh as a young child.
- God spoke to Samuel when the Word of the Lord was rarely heard.
- Samuel was a prophet and the last judge of Israel.
- Samuel warned the people about the cost of having a king.
- Samuel anointed both King Saul and King David.

Level 3

Create a card for The Twelve Spies.

- *Moses chose one man from each of the twelve tribes to go into the Promised Land and spy out the land for forty days.*
- *The spies found that the land was very good, the people were strong and the cities were fortified.*
- *When the children of Israel heard the report from the ten spies they rebelled against Moses and the other two spies.*
- *God punished the people for their rebellion: they would wander in the desert for forty years and all those twenty and older would die in the desert.*

Level 4

THE PROMISED LAND

Topical Bible

What is a *high place*?

Nave's, page 204

Bible Dictionary

What is a *covenant*?

Zondervan's, page 118

Concordance

One of the Ten Commandments is "You shall not make any *graven* images." Where is that verse found?

Exodus 20:4; Leviticus 26:1; Deuteronomy 5:8 (Cruden's, page 214)

Quest Question

Under what circumstances would God be justified in removing one set of people from a land and replacing them with His people?

If God had warned the people to repent of their sins and they refused to do so.

SP 94

THE PROMISED LAND

Timeline Review

Promised Land

The Exodus   *The Law*   The Tabernacle   *The Twelve Spies*

Bible Verses

Deuteronomy 8:2

Exodus 29:45

Deuteronomy 6:5

SP 95

THE PROMISED LAND

Background Bible Reading: Exodus 23-34; Numbers 33-35; Deuteronomy 2, 9
Time Frame: At the completion of the forty years in the desert

The Promise: *God reminded the Israelites that He had been with them in the wilderness and that He would be with them in the Promised Land. God promised that His angel would go before them as they entered and began the conquest of the land He had promised to Abraham, Isaac, and Jacob.*

Draw God with two warriors.

The Canaanites: *God removed the people who were living in the Promised Land, known then as Canaan, for two reasons. First, the people were to be removed because of their great wickedness in the sight of God. Second, the people were removed because God had promised the land of Canaan to Abraham, Isaac, and Jacob and their descendants after them.*

righteousness, wickedness   *Draw a man worshipping an idol and the Star of David.*

The Instructions: *God gave the Israelites three instructions regarding the people currently living in the land (Canaanites).*

No Covenants: *The Israelites were to make no covenants with the people who were in the land.*

covenants   *Draw two men shaking hands and a circle with a line through it.*

No People: *The Israelites were to drive all of the people completely out of the land.*

Draw a warrior chasing another man and a circle with a line through it.

No Idols/High Places: *The Israelites were to destroy all the idols and high places used by the people to worship false gods.*

idols, high places
    Draw a warrior on a high place with broken idols and a circle with a line through it.

©2005

THE PROMISED LAND

Bible Verses: Exodus 23-34; Numbers 33-35; Deuteronomy 2, 9
Time Frame: At the completion of the forty years in the desert

---

Deut. 2:7

Ex. 23:20

Deut. 9:3-5

The Promise

The Canaanites

Ex. 23:31-33

Num. 33:50-52

Ex. 34:10-13

No Covenants

No People

No Idols/High Places

SP 96

THE PROMISED LAND

The Warnings: *God warned the children of Israel in advance what would happen if they failed to obey His instructions.*

Conflict with the People: *If the children of Israel failed to remove the Canaanites, these people would become a constant source of conflict.*

 harass   *Draw two men fighting.*

Idol Worship: *If the children of Israel failed to remove all the Canaanites and to destroy all their idols, the remaining people and idols would tempt the Israelites to worship and serve false gods.*

 gods   *Draw a man bowing to an idol.*

The Division of the Promised Land among the Tribes: *The division of the Promised Land is recorded in Joshua 13-20. I recommend that you find a wall map that shows the division of the land among the twelve tribes.*

 (3) Location of the Twelve Tribes

The Levites: *Instead of receiving a portion of land as their inheritance, the Levites were given 48 cities throughout the Promised Land. Along with each city the Levites were given 2,000 cubits of land around the city for their flocks, herds, and crops.*

 inheritance   *Draw a square; label it "Levite city".*

1. When did the children of Israel enter the Promised Land? *After the forty years in the wilderness.*
2. What did God promise to do for the Israelites as they entered the Promised Land? *As He had been with them in the wilderness, He would be with them in the Promised Land.*
3. Why were the Canaanites removed from the land? *(1) God promised the land to Abraham, Isaac, and Jacob and their descendants and (2) the wickedness of the people living in Canaan.*
4. What instructions did God give the Israelites concerning the people in the land? *No covenants, no people, no idols or high places.*
5. What warnings did God give the Israelites? *If the Canaanites were left, they would be a source of constant conflicts and the Israelites would be tempted to worship false gods.*
6. How was the land divided? *By lot and according to the size of each tribe.*
7. Where were the Levites to live? *In cities throughout the Promised Land.*
8. What do we learn about God from these verses? *When God gives us instructions, He does so for our well-being. God fulfilled His promises to Abraham, Isaac, and Jacob.*

Num. 33:55-56

Conflict with the People

Ex. 23:33

Idol Worship

Num. 33:50-54

The Division of the Promised Land among the Tribes

Num. 35:2-8

48 Cities

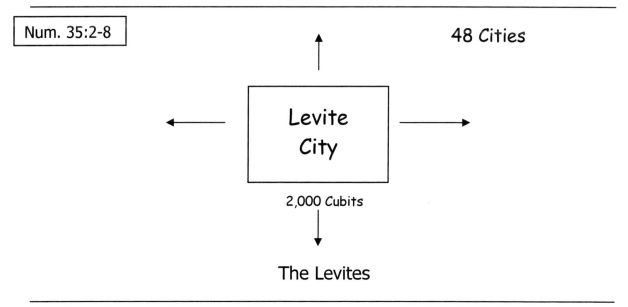

Levite
City

2,000 Cubits

The Levites

Lesson Review

1. When did the children of Israel enter the Promised Land?
2. What did God promise to do for the Israelites as they entered the Promised Land?
3. Why were the Canaanites removed from the land?
4. What instructions did God give the Israelites concerning the people in the land?
5. What warnings did God give the Israelites?
6. How was the land divided?
7. Where were the Levites to live?
8. What do we learn about God from these verses?

Memory Verse: Deuteronomy 1:8

SP 97

Level 3

Create a card for the Promised Land.

- *The Promised Land was given to Israel because of God's promised to Abraham, Isaac, and Jacob and because of the wickedness of the Canaanites living in the land.*
- *The Promised Land was a good land, with strong people and fortified cities.*
- *God gave the Israelites three instructions when entering the land:*
  1. *No covenants*
  2. *No people*
  3. *No high places or idols.*
- *The Promised Land was divided among the children of Israel.*

Level 4

THE JORDAN AND JERICHO

Topical Bible

What does the name *Jericho* mean?

Nave's, page 243

Bible Dictionary

Jericho is possibly the oldest city in the world? True or False

Zondervan's, page 275

Concordance

How many times is *Rahab* mentioned in Scripture?

9 times (Cruden's, page 391)

Quest Question

Why do you think the Lord God performed the miracle of drying up the Jordan River, similar to the miracle of drying up the Red Sea, for this generation of Israelites?

This generation of Israelites had grown up in the desert and heard the story of God parting the Red Sea from those who had witnessed this miracle. The generation that saw the Red Sea parting had died in the wilderness. God, here at the Jordan River, showed His mighty hand to this new generation as they entered the Promised Land. God was not only the God of Abraham, Isaac, Jacob, and Moses, but also their God.

SP 98

THE JORDAN AND JERICHO

Timeline Review

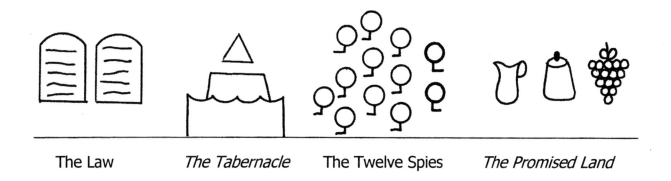

| The Law | *The Tabernacle* | The Twelve Spies | *The Promised Land* |

Bible Verses

Deuteronomy 1:8

Deuteronomy 8:2

Exodus 29:45

SP 99

THE JORDAN AND JERICHO

Background Bible Reading: Deuteronomy 34; Joshua 1-6
Time Frame: At the beginning of the conquest of the Promised Land

---

Moses Died: *After the forty years in the desert, the children of Israel again arrived at the border of the Promised Land. Moses was allowed to see the land and then died at the age of 120. God buried Moses in Moab.*

✧ (4) Israel, Mount Nebo   *Draw Moses' grave.*

Joshua, the New Leader: *Following the death of Moses, God chose Joshua to lead the children of Israel. Joshua, Moses' servant, had watched first-hand how Moses served God and led the children of Israel. God commanded Joshua to be strong and courageous as he took leadership of the children of Israel.*

Draw Joshua the warrior.

Rahab and the Two Spies: *Upon reaching the Jordan River, Joshua told the people to spend three days in preparation to enter the land. During this three-day period, Joshua sent two men to spy out the city of Jericho. The two spies were discovered to be in the city, but a harlot named Rahab hid them. In exchange for hiding the spies, they promised Rahab that when the Israelites attacked Jericho, she and her family would be spared if she followed their instructions.*

 harlot   *Draw Rahab and two men at the bottom of the wall.*

Crossing the Jordan River: *Following the three days of preparation on the east side of the Jordan River, Joshua instructed the people to follow the priest and the Levites. When the priest, who carried the ark of the covenant, stepped into the Jordan River, the water "stood up in a heap" and the children of Israel walked across the Jordan on dry ground.*

✧ (4) Jordan River

⌂ stood, heap   *Draw the priest carrying the ark and the waters parted.*

©2005

146

THE JORDAN AND JERICHO

Bible Verses: Joshua 1:1-6:20
Time Frame: At the beginning of the conquest of the Promised Land

---

Deut. 34:1-8

| Moses |

Moses Died

Josh. 1:1-3, 9

Joshua, the New Leader

Josh. 1:10-11

Josh. 2:1-15

Rahab and the Two Spies

Josh. 3:1-17

Crossing the Jordan River

SP 100

THE JORDAN AND JERICHO

Jericho—the First Six Days: *The first city that the children of Israel encountered after crossing the Jordan River was Jericho. God instructed Joshua to have all the men of war follow seven priests with trumpets and the Levites carrying the ark of the Covenant around Jericho. For six days this procession marched quietly around the city one time each day.*

✧ (4) Gilgal, Jericho   *Draw the priest with trumpets and the army marching around Jericho.*

Jericho—the Seventh Day: *On the seventh day the men of war, the priests, and the Levites carrying the ark marched around Jericho seven times.*

Draw the priest blowing trumpets and the men shouting.

Jericho Was Destroyed: *On the seventh time around the priests blew their trumpets, the men shouted, and the walls of Jericho fell down flat. When the walls came down, the men of Israel went in and took the city. Everyone in the city was killed, except Rahab and her family. The entire city was burnt, and the only thing, taken out of the city were the gold, silver, bronze, and iron, which were placed in the house of the Lord.*

⌂ trumpets, flat   *Draw two warriors on the flattened walls.*

---

1. Who was the leader of the children of Israel after Moses? *Joshua.*
2. Where did Moses die, and how was he buried? *Moab, and God buried him.*
3. Explain what happened when the children of Israel crossed the Jordan River. *When the Levites carrying the ark of the covenant entered the Jordan River, the water stood up in a heap, and the children of Israel walked across the river on dry ground.*
4. What was the first city the Israelites came to after crossing the Jordan River? *Jericho.*
5. How many days and how many times did they march around the city? *Seven days and thirteen times.*
6. What made the last march around Jericho different from all the others? *The men shouted and the priests blew their trumpets.*
7. What happened to the city on the seventh day? *The walls fell down flat, and the city was destroyed.*
8. What do we learn about God from these verses? *God can use unusual means to accomplish what He wants to do through us.*

©2005

148

Josh. 6:1-3, 6-7

Josh. 6:15-16

Jericho—the First Six Days

Josh. 6:17-19

Josh. 6:20-26

Jericho—the Seventh Day

Jericho was Destroyed

Lesson Review

1. Who was the leader of the children of Israel after Moses?
2. Where did Moses die, and how was he buried?
3. Explain what happened when the children of Israel crossed the Jordan River.
4. What was the first city the Israelites came to after crossing the Jordan River?
5. How many days and how many times did they march around the city?
6. What made the last march around Jericho different from all the others?
7. What happened to the city on the seventh day?
8. What do we learn about God from these verses?

Memory Verse: Joshua 4:23

SP 101

Level 3

Create a card for The Jordan and Jericho.

- *After the death of Moses, God appointed Joshua as leader.*
- *The Lord parted the Jordan River in order for the children of Israel to enter the Promised Land.*
- *Jericho was the first city that the children of Israel conquered in the Promised Land.*

Level 4

THE JUDGES

Topical Bible

What do you learn about the book of *Judges* and who the judges were?

Nave's, page 274

Bible Dictionary

Name the 13 *Judges* of Israel.
1. *Othniel*
2. *Ehud*
3. *Shamgar*
4. *Deborah and Barak*
5. *Gideon*
6. *Abimelech*
7. *Tola*
8. *Jair*
9. *Jephthah*
10. *Ibzan*
11. *Elon*
12. *Abdon*
13. *Samson*
(Zondervan's, page 301)

Concordance

In what book would you look for the story of *Gideon*?

Judges (Cruden's, page 195)

Quest Question

What does the term "they did what was right in their own eyes" imply?

They were not doing what was "right" in the eyes of God, by obeying His statutes, His commandments and His laws.

THE JUDGES

Timeline Review

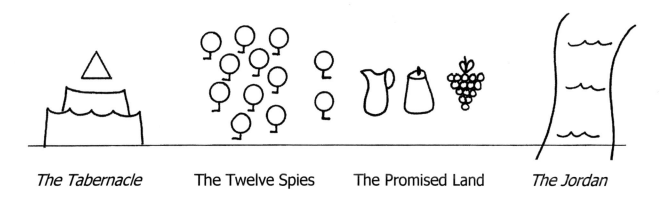

The Tabernacle　　　The Twelve Spies　　　The Promised Land　　　*The Jordan*

Bible Verses

Joshua 4:23

Deuteronomy 1:8

Deuteronomy 8:2

SP 103

THE JUDGES

Background Bible Reading: Joshua 24-Judges 21
Time Frame: The time of the judges

Joshua Died: *Joshua led the Israelites in their conquest of the Promised Land. The children of Israel followed Joshua until his death at 110 years of age. The people served the Lord as long as Joshua and the elders, who saw the works of the Lord, lived.*

Draw Joshua's grave.

The Cycle of the Judges: *In the book of Judges there is a cycle of Israel's relationship to God. Israel would follow the Lord until their leader/judge died, and then they would quickly* **rebel** *against God, turning to idolatry and those things that were "evil in the sight of the Lord." Then God allowed their enemies to defeat them, and after a time of* **bondage**, *the children of Israel would* **cry out** *to God in repentance. God would then send a* **judge** *to deliver them from their enemies and teach them how to walk in obedience to the Law. After the judge delivered them out of bondage, the land would usually have rest from war while that judge lived. The cycle of the judges is Rebel, Bondage, Cry Out, and Judge.*

 judge   *Draw the circular cycle of the judges.*

God Called Gideon: *When Deborah judged Israel, the land had rest from war for forty years. After her death the children of Israel did "evil in the sight of the Lord" and God turned them over to the attacks of the Midianites. The Israelites cried out to God, and God called Gideon to be their next judge. Gideon was threshing wheat when the angel of the Lord appeared to him to give him God's instructions.*

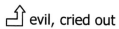 evil, cried out   *Draw the angel talking to Gideon.*

Gideon Called an Army: *The Midianite and Amalekite armies encamped near where Gideon lived. The Spirit of God came upon Gideon, and he called for an army from among the tribes of Manasseh, Asher, Zebulun, and Naphtali in order to attack the enemy armies.*

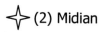 (2) Midian   *Draw a man blowing a trumpet and two men running with scrolls.*

THE JUDGES

Bible Verses: Judges 2-8, 21
Time Frame: The time of the judges

Jud. 2:7-9

Joshua

Elders

Joshua Died

Jud. 2:10-19

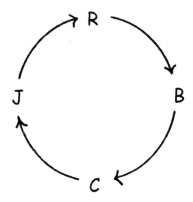

The Cycle of the Judges

Jud. 5:31

Jud. 6:1, 6-7, 11-16

Jud. 6:33-35

God Called Gideon

Gideon Called for an Army

SP 104

THE JUDGES

The Army Was Too Big: *Men came from the tribes Gideon summoned, totaling 32,000 warriors. God looked at the army and determined that it was too large. If Israel were to win this battle, they would be tempted to claim the glory for themselves, instead of giving the glory to God. Gideon told the warriors that if they were afraid or fearful, they should return home. Those who left numbered 22,000, leaving an army numbering 10,000.*

Draw Gideon talking to the army; one warrior stays but two are leaving.

The Army Was Tested: *God saw that the army was still too large, so He gave Gideon instructions about how to test the warriors. Gideon took the warriors to water and had them drink. The men who knelt down, putting their heads toward the water, were sent home. The men who knelt, scooped up water with their hands, and brought it to their mouths were the men chosen for the army. Gideon's army now numbered only 300.*

Draw one man at the water lapping and one with his face down in the water.

God Defeated Israel's Enemies: *Gideon equipped this small army with very interesting weapons: trumpets and torches, covered by a clay pots. In the middle of the night, Gideon's army surrounded the enemy's camp; they broke the jars, blew the trumpets, and shouted. God caused the enemy to be so confused by this that they killed each other.*

Draw Gideon and his men on a hill above a camp holding torches and trumpet.

The Time of the Judges: *After the death of Gideon, as before, the children of Israel began to worship idols. The book of Judges ends with the sad statement, "each man did what was right in his own eyes," but not what was right in the eyes of the Lord.*

right, eyes   *Draw God with eyes below and a man with eyes below.*

1. How old was Joshua when he died? *110 years old.*
2. What was the cycle Israel followed during the time of the judges? *Rebel/Bondage/Cry Out/Judge.*
3. What was Gideon doing when the Angel of the Lord appeared to him? *He was working, threshing wheat.*
4. Why did Gideon call an army? *To defeat the Midianite and Amalekite armies.*
5. At first how big was the army? *32,000 men.*
6. In the end how big was Gideon's army? *300 men and Gideon.*
7. What equipment did Gideon give his army? *Trumpets, and torches covered with clay pots.*
8. How were the Midianites defeated? *God confused them, and they killed one another.*
9. What do we learn about God from these verses? *God often waits until we cry out to Him before He delivers us.*

©2005

Jud. 7:2-3

Jud. 7:4-7

The Army Was Too Big

The Army Was Tested

Jud. 7:19-23

Jud. 21:25

Jud. 8:28, 33

Judges

God Defeated Israel's Enemies

The Time of the Judges

Lesson Review

1. How old was Joshua when he died?
2. What was the cycle Israel followed during the time of the judges?
3. What was Gideon doing when the Angel of the Lord appeared to him?
4. Why did Gideon call an army?
5. At first how big was the army?
6. In the end how big was Gideon's army?
7. What equipment did Gideon give his army?
8. How were the Midianites defeated?
9. What do we learn about God from these verses?

Memory Verse: Judges 21:25

SP 105

Level 3

Create a card for The Judges.

- *The time of the Judges was the time between the time of Joshua and the Kings.*
- *The cycle of the judges was: Rebellion, Bondage, Cry out, and Judge.*
- *One of the judges of Israel was Gideon.*
- *The times of the judges was a time when the children of Israel did what was right in their own eyes, instead of what was right in the sight of God's.*

Level 4

RUTH

Topical Bible

What does *Moab* mean?

> *Nave's, page 324*

Bible Dictionary

What is a *kinsman*?

> *Zondervan's, page 309*

What can you tell about the *redemption of land*?

> *Zondervan's, page 492*

Concordance

Give one Bible reference for the woman *Ruth*.

> *Answers will vary. (Cruden's, page 416)*

Quest Question

What does the term *kinsman redeemer* mean?

> *A near relative (kinsman) who had the right to buy back (redeem) land sold in a time of economic distress.*

RUTH

Timeline Review

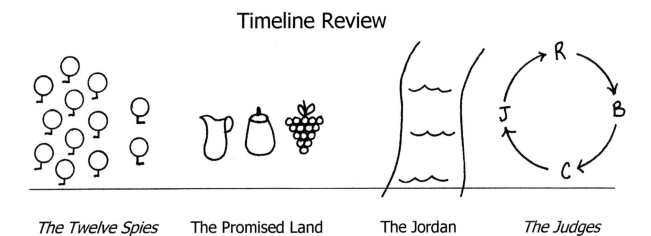

| *The Twelve Spies* | The Promised Land | The Jordan | *The Judges* |

Bible Verses

Judges 21:25

Joshua 4:23

Deuteronomy 1:8

SP 107

RUTH

Background Bible Reading: The Book of Ruth
Time Frame: The time of the judges

Ruth's Husband Died: *Naomi, her husband, and her sons left Bethlehem because of a famine and relocated in Moab. While in Moab, Naomi's husband died, and her sons married Moabite women. In time, both of Naomi's sons died, leaving her with her two widowed daughters-in-law.*

 (4) Israel, Moab

Elimelech, Mahlon, Chilion   *Draw three graves with one woman at each grave.*

Ruth and Naomi Left Moab: *Following the deaths of her sons, the widow Naomi decided to return home to Israel. At first Naomi wanted to take her daughters-in-law with her, but then she released them to return to their own families. Orpah, through tears, bid Naomi goodbye and returned to her family in Moab. Ruth refused to leave Naomi and confessed that not only did she want to go to Israel with Naomi, but she also wanted to serve Naomi's God, the God of Abraham, Isaac, and Jacob.*

Ruth, Naomi   *Draw Naomi and Ruth leaving for Israel, but Orpah returning to Moab.*

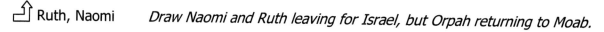

Ruth and Naomi in Israel: *The two women returned to Israel and settled in Bethlehem. They arrived in Bethlehem at the beginning of the barley harvest.*

 (4) Bethlehem   *Draw Ruth and Naomi at a table.*

RUTH

Bible Verses: The Book of Ruth
Time Frame: The time of the judges

Ruth 1:1-5

Ruth's Husband Died

Ruth 1:6-9, 14-18

Moab   Israel
←   →

Ruth 1:22

Bethlehem

 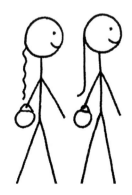

Ruth and Naomi Left Moab

Ruth and Naomi in Israel

SP 108

RUTH

Ruth Gleaned in Boaz's Field: *In order to eat, Naomi sent Ruth out to glean in the barley fields. Ruth began to glean in the field of a man named Boaz. Boaz took notice of Ruth and gave her extra grain. Ruth returned home to tell Naomi what happened.*

Boaz, glean   *Draw Ruth gleaning in the field and Boaz watching.*

Boaz, the Kinsman Redeemer: *Since Naomi's husband died, according to the Law his inheritance in Israel would fall to the nearest male relative (kinsman), who could then buy (redeem) the land (Lev. 25:23-38). Boaz approached the nearest kinsman at the city gate and inquired whether or not this man would redeem Naomi's land and marry Ruth, as required by the Law. The man refused to redeem the land and gave Boaz the right to redeem Naomi's land and to take Ruth as his wife.*

close relative, redeem   *Draw Boaz at the gate giving his sandal to another man.*

Boaz Married Ruth: *After redeeming the land of Naomi's husband, Boaz married Ruth.*

Draw Boaz and Ruth getting married.

Obed Was Born: *Boaz and Ruth had a son whom they named Obed. Obed became the grandfather of King David.*

Obed   *Draw Obed.*

1. Why did Ruth and Naomi leave Moab? *Because both their husbands were dead.*
2. Where did Ruth and Naomi live in Israel? *Bethlehem.*
3. What did Ruth do to help feed herself and Naomi? *Gleaned in the barley fields.*
4. What did Boaz have to do before he could marry Ruth? *Redeem Naomi's property.*
5. What was the name of the son born to Boaz and Ruth? *Obed.*
6. What do we learn about God from these verses? *God wants people of all nations to turn and serve Him, and when they do He provides for them.*

©2005

Ruth 2:1-9, 17-20

Ruth 4:1-9

Ruth Gleaned in Boaz's Field

Boaz, the Kinsman Redeemer

Ruth 4:10

Ruth 4:13, 17

Boaz Married Ruth

Obed Was Born

Lesson Review

1. Why did Ruth and Naomi leave Moab?
2. Where did Ruth and Naomi live in Israel?
3. What did Ruth do to help feed herself and Naomi?
4. What did Boaz have to do before he could marry Ruth?
5. What was the name of the son born to Boaz and Ruth?
6. What do we learn about God from these verses?

Memory Verse: Ruth 1:16

SP 109

Level 3

Create a card for Ruth.

- *Ruth was from Moab and lived at the time of the judges.*
- *Ruth moved with her mother-in-law, Naomi, from Moab to Israel after their husbands died.*
- *Boaz, a relative of Naomi, married Ruth.*
- *Boaz and Ruth had a son named Obed.*

Level 4

SAMUEL

Topical Bible

Who was *Hannah's* son?

Samuel, (Nave's, page 194)

Bible Dictionary

What was kept at *Shiloh* from the time of Joshua until the time of Samuel?

The Tabernacle (Zondervan's, page 547)

What does *Samuel* mean?

Zondervan's, page 521

Concordance

Give the reference for this verse: "they...brought the child to *Eli*."

I Samuel 1:25 (Cruden's, page 140)

Quest Question

How should we treat the Word of God?

Like Samuel did, letting none of God's Words "fall to the ground."

SP 110

SAMUEL

Timeline Review

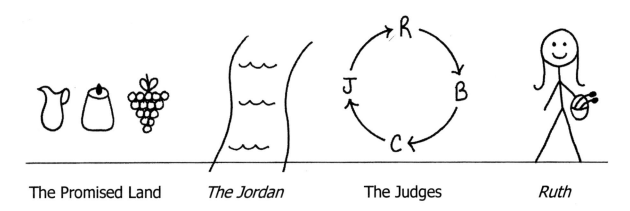

The Promised Land   *The Jordan*   The Judges   *Ruth*

Bible Verses

Ruth 1:16

Judges 21:25

Joshua 4:23

SP 111

SAMUEL

Background Bible Reading: I Samuel 1-8, 25
Time Frame: After the judges

Hannah Prayed for a Son: *Elkhanah had two wives, Hannah and Peninnah. Peninnah treated Hannah very badly because Hannah had no children. But Elkhanah loved Hannah and treated her very well. Once a year, Elkhanah took his whole family to Shiloh to worship the Lord. While there, Hannah prayed for a son and made a vow to God.*

✦ (4) Shiloh

 Shiloh, vow   *Draw Hannah praying.*

Hannah Gave Her Son to God: *Hannah returned home with her family and gave birth to a son whom she named Samuel. Hannah kept Samuel with her until he was weaned. Then she took him to Shiloh to serve God.*

Samuel, lent   *Draw Hannah and Elkhanah taking Samuel to Shiloh.*

Samuel Served the Lord: *Under the care of Eli, the priest at Shiloh, God blessed Samuel and he grew up serving the Lord. The Lord also blessed Hannah and Elkhanah with three more sons and two daughters.*

Draw Samuel following Eli the priest.

Samuel Heard God's Voice: *In a time when a word from the Lord was rare, God spoke to Samuel. God told Samuel that He was going to judge Eli's house because Eli had failed to judge his sons, who were involved in wicked acts. In contrast to Eli's sons, Samuel took the word of God seriously, and God was with him. As Samuel grew up, he "let none of God's words fall to the ground."*

fall to the ground   *Draw God speaking to Samuel.*

SAMUEL

Bible Verses: I Samuel 1:1-8; 2:11-21; 3:1-20; 7:15-17; 8:10-18; 25:1
Time Frame: After the judges

I Sam. 1:1-7, 10-11

Hannah Prayed for a Son

I Sam. 1:20-28; 2:11

Hannah Gave Her Son to God

I Sam. 2:18-21

Samuel Served the Lord

I Sam. 3:1-19

Samuel Heard God's Voice

©2005

SP 112

SAMUEL

Samuel: Prophet and Judge: *As a prophet of God in Israel, Samuel was an authorized spokesman for God, telling the Israelites what God wanted them to know. As a judge, Samuel oversaw some of the governing of Israel and ruled on various issues.*

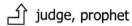 judge, prophet   *Draw Samuel as a judge and a prophet.*

Samuel Warned Israel: *Samuel continued through his lifetime to serve God and Israel, but as he grew old he placed his sons as judges in Israel, and they did evil. The elders of Israel came to Samuel complaining about his son's evil actions and asking that a king be appointed over Israel. Samuel prayed, and God told him to warn Israel about the cost of having a king. Samuel warned the Israelites, but they insisted on having a king to be like other nations.*

 (4) Bethel, Gilgal, Mizpah   *Draw Samuel talking to the children of Israel.*

Samuel Anointed Kings: *Samuel was the last judge of Israel and was the bridge between the time of the judges and the time of the kings. Samuel anointed the first two kings of Israel, Saul and David, before his death.*

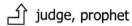 anointed   *Draw Samuel anointing Saul and David.*

Samuel Died: *During the reign of King Saul, Samuel died and the Israelites buried him at Ramah, his hometown.*

 (4) Ramah   *Draw Samuel's grave.*

---

1. What did Hannah pray for at Shiloh? *For God to give her a son.*
2. How did God answer Hannah's prayer? *God gave Hannah and Elkhanah a son.*
3. Why did Hannah take Samuel to Shiloh? *To give him to the Lord, as she had promised.*
4. What did Samuel do at Shiloh, at the tabernacle? *Samuel served the Lord under Eli the priest.*
5. In what positions did Samuel serve God and Israel? *As a prophet and a judge.*
6. What did Samuel warn Israel about having a king? *They would pay a high price for a king.*
7. What kings did Samuel anoint? *King Saul and King David.*
8. What do we learn about God from these verses? *God hears and answers prayer.*

©2005

I Sam. 3:20; 7:15-17

I Sam. 8:1-18

Prophet   Judge

Samuel: Prophet and Judge

Samuel Warned Israel

I Sam. 15:1; 16:13

I Sam. 25:1

Samuel Anointed Kings

Samuel

Samuel Died

Lesson Review

1. What did Hannah pray for at Shiloh?
2. How did God answer Hannah's prayer?
3. Why did Hannah take Samuel to Shiloh?
4. What did Samuel do at Shiloh, at the tabernacle?
5. In what positions did Samuel serve God and Israel?
6. What did Samuel warn Israel about having a king?
7. What kings did Samuel anoint?
8. What do we learn about God from these verses?

Memory Verse: I Samuel 3:19

©2005

SP 113

Review 4

1. When did the children of Israel enter the Promised Land? *After the forty years in the wilderness.*

2. What did God promise to do for the Israelites as they entered the Promised Land? *As He had been with them in the wilderness, He would be with them in the Promised Land.*

3. Why were the Canaanites removed from the land? *(1) God promised the land to Abraham, Isaac and Jacob and their descendants and (2) the wickedness of the people living in Canaan.*

4. What instructions did God give the Israelites concerning the people in the land? *No covenants, no people, no idols or high places.*

5. What warnings did God give the Israelites? *If the Canaanites were left, they would be a source of constant conflicts and the Israelites would be tempted to worship false gods.*

6. How was the Promised Land divided? *By lot and according to the size of tribe.*

7. Where did the Levites live? *In cities throughout the Promised Land.*

8. Recite Deuteronomy 1:8.

9. Who was the leader of the children of Israel after Moses? *Joshua.*

10. Where did Moses die, and how was he buried? *Moab, and God buried him.*

11. Explain what happened when the children of Israel crossed the Jordan River. *When the Levites carrying the Ark of the Covenant entered the Jordan River, the water stood up in a heap, and the children of Israel walked across the river on dry ground.*

12. What was the first city the Israelites came to after crossing the Jordan River? *Jericho.*

13. How many days and how many times did the Israelites march around Jericho? *Seven days and thirteen times.*

14. What made the last march around Jericho different from all the others? *The men shouted and the priests blew their trumpets.*

15. What happened to the city on the seventh day on the seventh march around Jericho? *The walls fell down flat and the city was destroyed.*

SP 114

16. Recite Joshua 4:23.

17. How old was Joshua when he died? *110 years old.*

18. What was the cycle Israel followed during the time of the judges?
Rebel/Bondage/Cry Out/Judge.

19. What was Gideon doing when the Angel of the Lord appeared to him? *He was working, threshing wheat.*

20. Why did Gideon call an army? *To defeat the Midianite and Amalekite armies.*

21. At first how big was the army? *32,000 men.*

22. In the end how big was the army? *300 men and Gideon.*

23. What equipment did Gideon give each member of his army? *A trumpet and a torch covered with a clay pot.*

24. How were the Midianites defeated? *God confused them, and they killed one another.*

25. Recite Judges 21:25.

26. Why did Ruth and Naomi leave Moab? *Because both their husbands were dead.*

27. Where did Ruth and Naomi live in Israel? *Bethlehem.*

28. What did Ruth do to help feed herself and Naomi? *Gleaned in the barley fields.*

29. What did Boaz have to do before he could marry Ruth? *Redeem Naomi's property.*

30. What was the name of the son born to Boaz and Ruth? *Obed.*

31. Recite Ruth 1:16.

32. What did Hannah pray for at Shiloh? *For God to give her a son.*

33. How did God answer Hannah's prayer? *God gave Hannah and Elkhanah a son.*

34. Why did Hannah take Samuel to Shiloh? *To give him to the Lord, as she had promised.*

35. What did Samuel do at Shiloh at the tabernacle? *Samuel served the Lord under Eli the priest.*

36. In what positions did Samuel serve God and Israel? *As a prophet and a judge.*

37. What did Samuel warn Israel about having a king? *The cost would be high.*

38. What kings did Samuel anoint? *King Saul and King David.*

39. Recite I Samuel 3:19.

SP 115

Section 6 Goals and Key Points

KING SAUL

The goal of this lesson is to look at the first king of Israel, Saul, and see that he served the Lord with a rebellious heart.

Key Points:
- Saul was appointed the first king of Israel when the Israelites demanded a king.
- Saul started out his reign as king by desiring to serve the Lord.
- Saul was disobedient to the Lord, and as a result the Spirit of God left him and a distressing spirit came upon him.
- Because of Saul's disobedience, God had Samuel anoint David as the next king of Israel.
- David served Saul by playing music to relieve him when the distressing spirit troubled him.
- Saul died when he was mortally wounded in battle and then fell on his own sword.

DAVID THE WARRIOR

The goal of this lesson is to look at the early life of David and how he served the Lord as a young man.

Key Points:
- David was of the godly lineage of Abraham.
- David was anointed by Samuel to be next king of Israel, even before King Saul died.
- As a young man David was a faithful shepherd, killing a lion and a bear to protect his father's sheep.
- David fought the Philistine giant, Goliath, and killed him.
- David became a popular military leader, but his popularity made King Saul jealous.
- King Saul sought to kill David, but David honored the Lord in his actions toward Saul.

DAVID THE KING

The goal of this lesson is to look at the reign of King David and how he served God with a faithful heart.

Key Points:
- David became king of Israel at the age of thirty and reigned forty years until his death.
- David conquered Jerusalem and called it the "City of David."
- David wanted to build the temple, but God told David the builder would be one of his sons.
- David sinned by numbering the fighting men of Israel, and as a result 70,000 men died.
- Although David could not build the temple, he made preparations for its building.
- David appointed his son, Solomon, as the next king of Israel before he died.

KING SOLOMON

The goal of this lesson is to look at the reign of Solomon and how he served the Lord with an unfaithful heart.

Key Points:
- Solomon became king of Israel after his father, David, died.
- God gave Solomon great wisdom and knowledge.
- Under Solomon, the nation of Israel was large and prosperous.
- Solomon built and dedicated the first temple to God.
- Solomon's sin and rebellion came when he married many foreign women and began to worship false gods.
- Solomon died after serving as king for forty years.

THE FIRST TEMPLE

The goal of this lesson is to study the building and dedication of the first temple in Jerusalem.

Key Points:
- The first temple was built on Mount Moriah in Jerusalem.
- The temple was a place where God dwelt among His people and where the people worshipped and offered sacrifices to God.
- The temple had specific furnishings that were similar to those of the tabernacle.

PSALMS AND PROVERBS

The goal of this lesson is to introduce your students to the books of Psalms and Proverbs.

Key Points:
- Psalms were written for the purpose of worshipping God.
- King David wrote many of the psalms.
- Proverbs are wise sayings.
- King Solomon wrote many of the proverbs.

Level 3

Create a card for Samuel.

- *Samuel was the son born to Hannah after she had prayed for a son.*
- *Samuel was taken to Shiloh and grew up serving in the tabernacle under Eli the priest.*
- *God spoke to Samuel.*
- *Samuel was a prophet and a judge of Israel.*
- *Samuel anointed two kings: Saul and David.*

Level 4

KING SAUL

Topical Bible

What tribe of Israel was *Saul* from?

Benjamin. (Nave's, page 427)

Bible Dictionary

What is an *armor bearer*?

Zondervan's, page 55

Concordance

What is the first reference to *king* in the Bible?

Genesis 14:18 (Cruden's, page 271)

Quest Question

Which does God prefer, our obedience or our sacrifices? Explain your answer.

Obedience; I Samuel 15:22.

SP 116

KING SAUL

Timeline Review

| The Jordan | *The Judges* | Ruth | *Samuel* |

Bible Verses

I Samuel 3:19

Ruth 1:16

Judges 21:25

SP 117

KING SAUL

Background Bible Reading: I Samuel 8-31; II Samuel 1
Time Frame: The time of the kings

Israel Demanded a King: *When Samuel was old, he appointed his sons as judges in Israel. The elders of Israel saw that Samuel's sons did evil, so they asked Samuel to appoint a king over Israel. Although Samuel warned the children of Israel about the high cost of having a king, they still insisted that they wanted to be like other countries and have a king.*

Draw the elders talking to Samuel.

Saul Chosen as the First King: *The Lord brought Saul to Samuel, and Samuel anointed him as king. Samuel called all Israel together and revealed to them, by lot, who was to be the first king of Israel. Saul appealed to the Israelites because of his appearance; he was very tall and very good-looking.*

 anointed   *Draw Samuel crowing Saul as king.*

Saul was Disobedient to God: *Saul began his reign as king by desiring to do what was right before the Lord. As Saul began his second year as king, the army of Israel was called together to fight against the Philistines. Samuel had told Saul to wait seven days, at which time Samuel would come and offer the sacrifices. Saul became impatient and took it upon himself to offer the sacrifices instead of waiting for Samuel, the one appointed by God to make sacrifices. This displeased God, and God told Saul He was going to choose another king, a man after God's own heart, to be the next king. In another incident, the Lord told Saul to completely defeat and destroy the Amalekites. Saul failed to kill the king and then kept the best of the livestock for "sacrifices." God again was displeased and told Saul that He desired obedience rather than sacrifice. God regretted that He had made Saul king because of his disobedient heart.*

 burnt offering, regretted

Draw Samuel coming to the altar with Saul holding a torch /Saul with treasures behind him.

KING SAUL

Bible Verses: I Samuel 9:1-31:6
Time Frame: The time of the kings

I Sam. 8:1-5, 9, 19-22

I Sam. 9:1-2, 27

I Sam. 10:1, 17-24

Israel Demanded a King

Saul Chosen as the First King

I Sam. 13:1-14

I Sam. 15:3, 9, 17-26, 35

Saul Was Disobedient to God

SP 118

KING SAUL

David Anointed to Be King: *The Lord sent Samuel to the house of Jesse and anointed Jesse's youngest son to be the next king of Israel. David was not chosen because of his height or good looks, but because of his desire to serve the Lord obediently. The Spirit of the Lord came upon David and was with him from that point on.*

 rejected   *Draw Samuel crowing David as king.*

God's Spirit Departed from Saul: *The Spirit of the Lord departed from Saul, and instead a distressing spirit plagued him.*

 distressing spirit   *Draw the Spirit departing and a distressing spirit coming on Saul.*

David Served Saul: *Saul's servants suggested music to relieve the distressing spirit. One servant recommended David because he was a skillful musician and a man of valor. David was then recruited to serve Saul.*

Draw Saul with the distressing spirit and David playing music.

Saul's Death: *Saul continued as king of Israel, and during a battle with the Philistines he was mortally injured and all his sons were killed. Saul requested that his armorbearer kill him, but the armorbearer refused, so Saul fell on his own sword and died. King Saul served Israel a total of forty years.*

 armorbearer   *Draw Saul's grave.*

---

1. Whom did Samuel anoint as the first king of Israel? *Saul.*
2. What tribe of Israel was King Saul from? *Benjamin.*
3. How did King Saul serve God? *With a disobedient heart.*
4. What happened to King Saul when he was disobedient to God? *The Spirit of God departed from him, and a distressing spirit came upon him.*
5. How did King Saul get relief from his distressing spirit? *By having David play music for him.*
6. Who was anointed king before King Saul died? *David.*
7. How did King Saul die? *By falling on his own sword.*
8. What do we learn about God from these verses? *God's greatest desire is for our obedience.*

©2005

I Sam. 16:1-13

I Sam. 16:14

David Anointed to Be King

God's Spirit Departed from Saul

I Sam. 16:15-18, 23

I Sam. 31:1-6

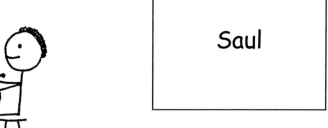

David Served Saul

Saul's Death

Lesson Review

1. Who did Samuel anoint as the first king of Israel?
2. What tribe of Israel was King Saul from?
3. How did King Saul serve God?
4. What happened to King Saul when he was disobedient to God?
5. How did King Saul get relief from his distressing spirit?
6. Who was anointed king before King Saul died?
7. How did King Saul die?
8. What do we learn about God from these verses?

Memory Verse: I Samuel 16:7

SP 119

Level 3

Create a card for King Saul.

- *King Saul was the first king of Israel.*
- *King Saul began his reign serving God but soon afterward disobeyed God.*
- *God's Spirit left Saul after his acts of disobedience and a distressing spirit was given to him.*
- *Saul served as the king of Israel for forty years.*

Level 4

DAVID THE WARRIOR

Topical Bible

What does the name *Goliath* mean and where was he from?

> *Nave's, pages 184-185*

Bible Dictionary

What does *defile* mean?

> *Zondervan's, page 130*

Concordance

How often are giants mentioned in the Bible?

> *10 times (Cruden's, page 195)*

Quest Question

What does being faithful in the "little things" of life prepare us for?

> *Being faithful in the "big things" of life. David was faithful in his job as a shepherd, killing a bear and a lion when no one was looking or would know what he had done. His obedience enabled him to be able to kill Goliath when the king and the army of Israel were watching.*

SP 120

DAVID THE WARRIOR

Timeline Review

The Judges   *Ruth*   Samuel   *Saul*

Bible Verses

I Samuel 16:7

I Samuel 3:19

Ruth 1:16

SP 121

DAVID THE WARRIOR

Background Bible Reading: I Samuel 16-24
Time Frame: The time of the kings

David's Family: *Adam, Noah, Shem, Abraham, Isaac, Jacob, Judah, Boaz, Obed, Jesse, David. Ten generations from Adam to Noah, ten generations from Noah to Abraham and fourteen generations from Abraham to David, thirty-four generations in all.*

Draw David's family line.

David Anointed to Be King: *Although Saul was the king of Israel, God's Spirit had departed from him. God chose David as king, and Samuel anointed him to be the next king of Israel.*

 (5) Bethlehem   *Draw Samuel crowing David as king.*

David Was a Shepherd: *David had been sent by his father to take food to his brothers who were with King Saul and the Israelite army facing the Philistines. When David heard and saw what Goliath was saying and doing, he volunteered to go fight Goliath. King Saul questioned David's ability to fight Goliath until David told him how he had killed a lion and a bear while tending his father's flocks. Saul blessed David and then allowed him to go fight Goliath.*

 (5) Philistia, Gath

Draw David between a bear and a lion.

David Killed Goliath: *David did not go to battle relying upon his own strength and ability but upon the name of the Lord and the fact that the Lord would go with him. With sling in hand and Goliath's mocking words ringing in his ear, David threw the stone, and Goliath fell down dead.*

defied   *Draw David and Goliath.*

DAVID THE WARRIOR

Bible Verses: I Samuel 16:1-24:20
Time Frame: The time of the kings

Ruth 4:21-22

Adam
Noah
Shem
Abraham
Isaac
Jacob
Judah
Boaz
Obed
Jesse
David

David's Family

I Sam. 16:1, 6-13

David Anointed to Be King

I Sam. 17:33-37

David Was a Shepherd

I Sam. 17:44-50

David Killed Goliath

SP 122

DAVID THE WARRIOR

Saul's Jealousy of David: *Following the victory over Goliath, David led the army of Israel against the Philistines. When he returned from battle, the women sang David's praises.*

 behaved wisely   *Draw women singing, David walking, and Saul watching.*

Saul Tried to Kill David: *Saul heard the women singing about David and became suspicious and distressed. Upon returning, David went to play music for Saul because he was distressed. Instead of listening to David play, King Saul threw a spear at him and tried to kill him. Although Saul treated David badly, David continued to behave wisely before Saul, and the Lord blessed him.*

 eyed   *Draw Saul throwing a spear at David.*

David's Battle with Saul: *King Saul knew that David was chosen by God to be the next king of Israel. Saul feared David because the Spirit of God was with David and had departed from Saul. David fled after Saul repeatedly attempted to kill him. Saul pursued David and his men. At one time David's men were hiding in a cave, and Saul came in to relieve himself. David was close enough to cut off a corner of Saul's robe. God convicted David about cutting the robe, and David made it known to Saul that he could have killed him, but he didn't. Saul recognized what David had done, and they departed from one another in peace, for a time.*

 robe   *Draw David cutting Saul's robe/David on a hill talking to Saul.*

---

1. What was David's family line? *Adam, Noah, Shem, Abraham, Judah, Boaz, Obed, Jesse.*
2. Who anointed David king of Israel? *Samuel.*
3. What and who did David kill as a young man? *A lion, a bear, and the giant Goliath.*
4. Why was King Saul jealous of David? *The people loved David, and God's Spirit was with him.*
5. What did King Saul try to do to David? *Kill him.*
6. What was David's response to Saul's attempts to kill him? *He fled from Saul but continued to do what was wise and right in the eyes of the Lord.*
7. What do we learn about God from these verses? *God desires for us to behave wisely and do what is right, even when people are trying to hurt us. The Lord always rewards integrity and honesty.*

I Sam. 18:5-7

I Sam. 18:8-16

Saul's Jealously of David

Saul Tried to Kill David

I Sam. 24:1-7

I Sam. 24:8-10, 15-20

David's Battle with Saul

Lesson Review

1. What was David's family line?
2. Who anointed David king of Israel?
3. What and who did David kill as a young man?
4. Why was King Saul jealous of David?
5. What did King Saul try to do to David?
6. What was David's response to Saul's attempts to kill him?
7. What do we learn about God from these verses?

Memory Verse: I Samuel 18:14

SP 123

Level 3

Create a card for King David.

- *David was a shepherd as a young man, and he killed a lion and a bear.*
- *David killed the Philistine giant Goliath.*
- *David led the army of Israel into many successful battles.*

Level 4

DAVID THE KING

Topical Bible

Give at least five other names by which *Jerusalem* was known.

Nave's, page 244

Bible Dictionary

What was a *threshing floor,* and where were they built?

Zondervan's, page 584

Concordance

David was called "a man after God's *own heart.*" What is the reference for this saying?

I Samuel 13:14. (Cruden's, page 232)

Quest Question

What should we do when we sin?

I John 1:9. Acknowledge that what we did was sin, repent, ask God for forgiveness, ask those we have hurt or offended for forgiveness, and make restitution when necessary.

SP 124

DAVID THE KING

Timeline Review

Ruth   *Samuel*   Saul   *David*

Bible Verses

I Samuel 18:14

I Samuel 16:7

I Samuel 3:19

SP 125

DAVID THE KING

Background Bible Reading: II Samuel 1-7; I Chronicles 20-30
Time Frame: The time of the kings

David Established as King: *After the death of King Saul there was some disagreement about who would become the next king of Israel. Finally, all the tribes came together to make David the king over all of Israel. David was thirty years old at this time.*

Draw David receiving his crown.

David Conquered Jerusalem: *King David and his men went up against the Jebusites who held Jerusalem, which was a strongly fortified city. After the city of Jerusalem was conquered, it became known as the "City of David." God was with David, and he became great.*

 (5) Jerusalem   *Draw David at the gate of Jerusalem.*

David and the House for the Ark: *God had blessed David as king and had given Israel rest from war under his leadership. As David sat in his own house, he had the desire to build a permanent home for the ark of God. At first Nathan the prophet agreed. God then spoke to Nathan, telling him that David would not be the one to build the permanent dwelling place for the ark of God. Instead, God promised David that his son would be the one to build the temple.*

 house   *Draw David thinking about the house for the ark of God.*

David Numbered the Men: *David was a good king of Israel and a "man after God's own heart," but he was also a man like us, who sinned. David decided to number the fighting men of Israel, trusting in the strength of his army instead of the God of Israel. God was displeased with this action.*

number   *Draw David numbering men.*

DAVID THE KING

Bible Verses: II Samuel 5:1-7:13; I Chronicles 21:1-29:28
Time Frame: The time of the kings

II Sam. 5:1-5

II Sam. 5:6-7, 9-10

David Established as King

David Conquered Jerusalem

II Sam. 7:1-13

I Chron. 21:1-7

David and the House for the Ark

David Numbered the Men

SP 126

DAVID THE KING

The Consequences: *David realized and repented of his sin (counting the fighting men), but the consequences still had to be paid. David was asked to choose between three options. He chose among three days of plague, in which 70,000 men of Israel died. When the plague was stopped, it was at the threshing floor of Ornan, the Jebusite. David bought the property to erect an altar, and offered sacrifices to the Lord. (This location would be used by Solomon to build the temple, II Chron. 3:1.)*

plague, sackcloth   *Draw David and the men who died.*

Temple Preparations: *Although David could not build the temple; he made abundant preparations for its building before his death.*

Draw David with materials and a sketch of the temple.

Solomon Was Appointed King: *David remembered God's promise to him, and before he died he made Solomon the next king of Israel.*

Draw David crowning Solomon as king.

David Died: *David reigned over Israel forty years and died at age seventy.*

Draw David's grave.

1. How old was David when he became king of Israel? *Thirty.*
2. What city did David conquer which was later called the "City of David"? *Jerusalem.*
3. What did David want to build for God? *The house for the ark of God (the temple).*
4. What sin of David's did we read about in this lesson? *Numbering the army, trusting in man.*
5. What were the consequences of David's sin? *70,000 men died.*
6. How did David make preparations for the temple? *By gathering materials.*
7. Which son of David's was appointed as king after David? *Solomon.*
8. How long did David reign as king of Israel? *Forty years.*
9. What do we learn about God from these verses? *God punishes our sin, and our sins often affect other people.*

I Chron. 21:11-17, 27, 28

I Chron. 22:1-5

I Chron. 29:1-4

70,000 died
The Consequences

Temple Preparations

II Sam. 7:12-13

I Chron. 23:1

I Chron. 29:26-28

David

Solomon Was Appointed King

David Died

Lesson Review

1. How old was David when he became king of Israel?
2. What city did David conquer which was later called the "City of David"?
3. What did David want to build for God?
4. What sin of David's did we read about in this lesson?
5. What were the consequences of David's sin?
6. How did David make preparations for the temple?
7. Which son of David's was appointed as king after David?
8. How long did David reign as king of Israel?
9. What do we learn about God from these verses?

Memory Verse: II Samuel 8:15

SP 127

Level 3

Add to the King David card.

- *David was the second king of Israel.*
- *King David was known as a man after God's own heart, although he sinned and he always repented of his sin.*
- *David served as the king of Israel for forty years.*

Level 4

KING SOLOMON

Topical Bible

What does the name *Solomon* mean?

> *Nave's, page 457*

Bible Dictionary

What is a *concubine*?

> *Zondervan's, page 116*

Concordance

If you were researching *Solomon*, with what verse would you begin?

> *II Samuel 5:14 (Cruden's, page 457)*

Quest Question

Why should you consider the religious beliefs of the person you desire to date or marry?

> *Answers will vary. Use Solomon's life as an example, I Kings 11:1-6.*

SP 128

KING SOLOMON

Timeline Review

Samuel   Saul   *David*

Bible Verses

II Samuel 8:15

I Samuel 18:14

I Samuel 16:7

SP 129

KING SOLOMON

Background Bible Reading: II Chronicles 1-9; I Kings 1-11
Time Frame: The time of the kings

Solomon Became King: *King David died after serving as king of Israel for forty years, and before his death he appointed Solomon as the next king of Israel.*

Draw David making Solomon king.

Solomon's Request: *Shortly after Solomon became king he went to the tabernacle to offer a burnt offering. The Lord appeared to Solomon and asked Solomon what He should give him. Solomon requested wisdom and knowledge, to know how to lead the people God had given him to rule over. God granted his request plus riches, wealth, and honor above all kings before and after him.*

 wisdom, knowledge   *Draw Solomon praying at the altar.*

Solomon's Wisdom: *As God promised, He gave Solomon wisdom and knowledge and soon his fame spread to the surrounding nations.*

Draw Solomon with animals and flowers.

Israel under Solomon: *While King Solomon was king, Israel expanded the amount of land it controlled. The land also had rest from war.*

 (5) Beersheba, Dan, kingdom of Israel   *Draw "Israel" with arrows going out.*

Solomon's Riches: *A very large amount of food was needed each day for the king and his guests. Solomon collected taxes from both the Israelites and people traveling through Israel on the major trade routes between Mesopotamia and Egypt. People traveled to see Solomon and brought him precious and unique gifts.*

Draw money, horses and a table with food.

Solomon's Writings: *Solomon spoke 3,000 proverbs and wrote 1,005 songs during his lifetime. Solomon also spoke about trees, plants, and animals with such wisdom and knowledge that men from other countries went to Israel to hear Solomon speak.*

Draw a song book and another book.

KING SOLOMON

Bible Verses: I Kings 2:10-11:43
Time Frame: The time of the kings

| I Kings 2:10-12 | II Chron. 1:6-12 |

Knowledge

Wisdom

Solomon Became King   Solomon's Request

| I Kings 4:29-30 | I Kings 4:20, 24-25 |

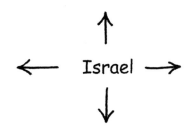

Solomon's Wisdom   Israel under Solomon

| I Kings 4: 22-23; 10:14, 23-27 | I Kings 4:32-34 |

 3,000 Proverbs

 1,005 Songs

Solomon's Riches   Solomon's Writings

SP 130

KING SOLOMON

Solomon and the First Temple: *Solomon acknowledged God's fulfilled promises to David: Solomon, David's son, was the king of Israel and the temple was completed.*

 temple   *Draw Solomon watching the temple being built.*

The Dedication of the Temple: *When the temple was completed, Solomon and the children of Israel gathered and dedication it. God made His presence known by consuming the sacrifices and offerings with fire from heaven, and His glory filled the temple.*

 glory   *Draw Solomon praising the Lord before the temple and the altar.*

Solomon's Sin: *Solomon had 700 wives and 300 concubines, which was in disobedience to God's law forbidding multiple marriages (Deut. 17:17) and marriage to anyone who did not worship the God of Israel (Deut. 7:1-4). Solomon compounded his sin by turning from the God of Israel, who had appeared to him twice, and by worshipping false gods. These things were evil in the sight of God and showed that Solomon had an unfaithful heart toward God. Because of Solomon's disobedience, the nation would be torn away from his son after his death.*

 high places, concubines   *Draw Solomon with women and him bowing at a high place.*

Solomon's Death: *Solomon died after being king of Israel for forty years.*

Draw Solomon's grave

1. Who was the third king of Israel? *Solomon.*
2. What did Solomon ask for from God? *Wisdom and knowledge.*
3. What was Israel like when Solomon was king? *United, very large, and prosperous.*
4. What did Solomon write? *3,000 proverbs and 1,005 songs.*
5. What did Solomon build that David was not allowed to build? *The temple.*
6. What was Solomon's sin? *Worshipping false gods, having multiple wives and marrying foreign women.*
7. How long did Solomon rule Israel? *Forty years.*
8. What do we learn about God from these verses? *God wants us to worship Him throughout our lifetime and not worship or serve any other gods.*

I Kings 8:17-21

I Kings 8:22-23, 54, 55, 62, 63

II Chron. 7:1-4

Solomon and the First Temple

The Dedication of the Temple

I Kings 3:1-3; 11:1-6, 9-13

I Kings 11:41-43

Solomon's Sin

Solomon

Solomon's Death

Lesson Review

1. Who was the third king of Israel?
2. What did Solomon ask for from God?
3. What was Israel like when Solomon was king?
4. What did Solomon write?
5. What did Solomon build that David was not allowed to build?
6. What was Solomon's sin?
7. How long did Solomon rule Israel?
8. What do we learn about God from these verses?

Memory Verse: I Kings 11:6

SP 131

Level 3

Create a card for King Solomon.

- *King Solomon was the third king of Israel.*
- *God gave Solomon wisdom and knowledge, riches and honor.*
- *King Solomon began his reign serving God, but he married many women who led him to worship false gods.*
- *Solomon built and dedicated the first temple.*
- *Solomon served as the king of Israel for forty years.*

Level 4

THE FIRST TEMPLE

Topical Bible

What other names is the *temple* known by?

Nave's, page 475

Bible Dictionary

What two important events took place on Mount *Moriah*? What was built on Mount Moriah?

Zondervan's, page 376

Concordance

If you were researching the *vessels* (furnishings) that were in the temple, what verse would you begin with?

II Chronicles 36:7 (Cruden's, page 493)

Quest Question

Why do you think the temple was needed to replace the tabernacle?

The tabernacle was a mobile place of worship for the children of Israel while they were in the desert, through the time of Solomon. However, when Israel established a capital city, a permanent place of worship was needed.

SP 132

THE FIRST TEMPLE

Timeline Review

Saul   David   *Solomon*

Bible Verses

I Kings 11:6

II Samuel 8:15

I Samuel 18:14

SP 133

THE FIRST TEMPLE

Background Bible Reading: I Kings 5- 8; II Chronicles 2-7
Time Frame: King Solomon's reign

The Temple's Location: *The location for the temple of God was on Mount Moriah. This was the very threshing floor that David bought to offer sacrifices to God. This location is also believed to be the area where Abraham went to offer his son Isaac to God (Gen.22:2).*

 threshing floor   *Draw the temple on a hill, label Mount Moriah.*

The Time of Building: *The building of the temple began in the fourth year of King Solomon's reign (480 years after the children of Israel left Egypt). It took seven years to build the temple.*

Draw the completed temple and note seven years.

The Purpose of the Temple: *The temple replaced the tabernacle as the central place of worship and sacrifice for the children of Israel. Like the tabernacle, the temple was the place in which God dwelt among His people. The temple was also a reminder to the children of Israel that they were to be obedient to all the laws of the Lord.*

statutes, judgments, commandments

Draw the temple, with God above and people worshipping and sacrificing.

The Size of the Temple: *The temple measured sixty cubits in length, twenty cubits in width, and thirty cubits in height. This was much larger than the tabernacle.*

cubit   *Draw a rectangle and the temple measurements.*

THE FIRST TEMPLE

Bible Verses: I Kings 6-7; II Chronicles 3, 7
Time Frame: King Solomon's reign

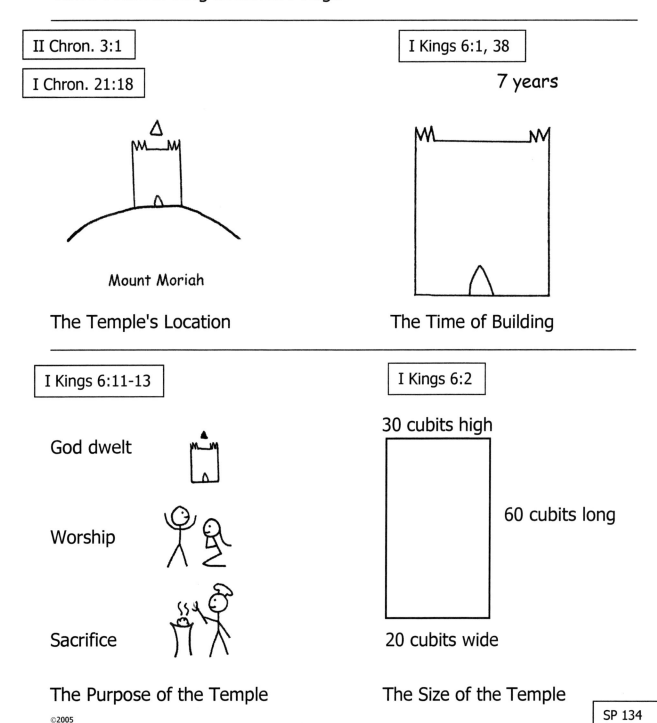

II Chron. 3:1

I Chron. 21:18

Mount Moriah

The Temple's Location

I Kings 6:1, 38

7 years

The Time of Building

I Kings 6:11-13

God dwelt

Worship

Sacrifice

The Purpose of the Temple

I Kings 6:2

30 cubits high

60 cubits long

20 cubits wide

The Size of the Temple

SP 134

THE FIRST TEMPLE

Furnishings of the Temple: *The temple had the same furnishings as the tabernacle: the ark of the Covenant, the altar of incense, the table of showbread, ten lampstands (the tabernacle only had one), the bronze laver, and the altar of burnt offerings. (Note: It is believed that the tabernacle itself may have been stored somewhere in the temple or its storage rooms.)*

Draw and label the various furnishings of the temple.

The Dedication of the Temple: *Kneeling before all Israel and the Lord, King Solomon praised God. When he had finished praying, fire from heaven came down and consumed the burnt offerings and sacrifices. The glory of the Lord then filled the temple. God's presence had come to dwell in the temple, among the children of Israel.*

Draw Solomon dedicating the temple.

The Layout of the Temple: *See drawings on the next page. I recommend that you do your own study on the various furnishings of the temple and the courtyard.*

Draw furnishing in the temple.

---

1. Where was the temple of the Lord built (include city)? *Mt. Moriah, Jerusalem, Israel.*
2. How long did it take to build the temple? *Seven years.*
3. What was the purpose of the temple? *(1) A place for God to dwell among His people and (2) a place of worship and sacrifice for the children of Israel.*
4. Give the size of the temple. *Sixty cubits in length, twenty in width, and thirty in height.*
5. What was in the temple? *The Ark of the Covenant, the altar of incense, the table of showbread, and ten menorahs or lampstands.*
6. How was the temple dedicated to God? *With Solomon praying, the people worshipping, and God responding with fire from heaven and His glory filled the temple.*
7. What do we learn about God from these verses? *God desires to dwell among His people.*

I Kings 7:47-51

II Chron. 7:1-4

 Ark of the Covenant

 Altar of Incense

 Table of Showbread

 Lampstands

Temple Furnishings

The Dedication of the Temple

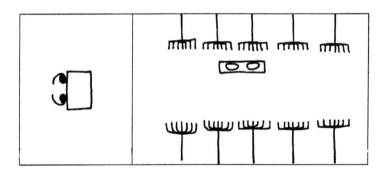

The Layout of the Temple

Lesson Review

1. Where was the temple of the Lord built (include city)?
2. How long did it take to build the temple?
3. What was the purpose of the temple?
4. Give the size of the temple.
5. What was in the temple?
6. How was the temple dedicated to God?
7. What do we learn about God from these verses?

Memory Verse: I Kings 6:13

SP 135

Level 3

Create a card for The First Temple.

- *The first temple was built by King Solomon.*
- *The temple was built on Mount Moriah, in Jerusalem.*
- *The temple took seven years to build.*
- *God skilled and gifted men to build the Temple.*
- *The Temple was a place where God dwelt among His people, a place of worship and sacrifice.*
- *The Temple was dedicated by Solomon and the children of Israel.*

Level 4

PSALMS AND PROVERBS

Topical Bible

What is a *rod*?

Nave's, page 413

Bible Dictionary

Psalms is the longest book of the Bible. True or False

True. (Zondervan's. page 479)

Concordance

"The Lord is my *shepherd.*" Give the reference.

Psalms 23:1 (Cruden's, page 441)

Quest Question

Why does the Lord compare Himself to a shepherd?

Answers will vary.

PSALMS AND PROVERBS

Timeline Review

Saul   *David*   Solomon   *First Temple*

Bible Verses

I Kings 6:13

I Kings 11:6

II Samuel 8:15

SP 137

PSALMS AND PROVERBS

Background Bible Reading: Psalms and Proverbs
Time Frame: The Time of the kings

The book of Psalms contains *songs* written for *worshipping God*.

King *David* wrote many of the Psalms.

I recommend sharing your favorite Psalms and Proverbs with your students, telling them why they are your favorite and what God has taught you through them.

Verse 1: *God, like the shepherd, provides us with food. God watches out for our protection and takes care of our needs. God is not far off, but near us; the shepherd lived with his sheep.*

Draw a shepherd with a sheep.

Verse 2: *Green pastures and still waters are scarce in Israel, so the shepherd had to know the area so well that he could lead the sheep to places of food and water.*

Draw a sheep at water.

Verse 3: *The shepherd would frequently move his sheep in order for them to have enough food and water. The sheep had to learn to trust the shepherd to lead them.*

Draw a sheep following the shepherd.

Verse 4: *Many times in our lives death will come near us; either our lives will be endangered or a loved one will die, but we can be sure that God is with us. The rod was used for correction, to keep the sheep out of danger and on the right path.*

 rod, staff   *Draw a sheep in a valley.*

Verse 5: *God gives us what we need when we face our enemies, and He is the one who makes us successful.*

Draw the shepherd guarding the sheep.

Verse 6: *Mercy and goodness will mark the life of a person who chooses to follow God throughout his lifetime.*

Draw a sheep walking on a path.

PSALMS AND PROVERBS

Bible Verses: Psalms and Proverbs
Time Frame: The time of the Kings

The book of Psalms contains *songs* written for *worshipping God.*

King *David* wrote many of the Psalms.

Psalm 23

PSALMS AND PROVERBS

The book of *Proverbs* is a book of *wise sayings.*

King *Solomon* wrote many of the Proverbs.

Proverbs 3:5 *Trusting in the Lord is the opposite of trusting in yourself.*

Fill in the chart.

Proverbs 3:6 *When given the opportunity, we should acknowledge God's work in our lives. We also need to pray that God would direct us in the way we are to go.*

paths

Fill in the chart.

Proverbs 3:27 *If you know of a need and can meet that need, you should.*

Draw a man praying

Proverbs 15:3 *God sees everything, whether it is good or bad.*

Draw God seeing the "Good" and "Evil"

Teachers: If time permits, have your students write their own psalm or proverb.

The book of *Proverbs* is a book of *wise sayings.*

King *Solomon* wrote many of the Proverbs.

Proverbs

Pro. 3:5-6

You do	God will
Trust in the Lord	*God will direct your path*
Lean not on your understanding	
Acknowledge God in all your ways	

Pro. 3:27

Pro. 15:3

Evil

Good

Memory Verse: Proverbs 3:5-6

SP 139

Review 5

1. Whom did Samuel anoint as the first king of Israel? *Saul.*

2. What tribe of Israel was King Saul from? *Benjamin.*

3. How did King Saul serve God? *With a disobedient heart.*

4. What happened to King Saul when he was disobedient to God? *The Spirit of God departed from him, and a distressing spirit came upon him.*

5. How did King Saul get relief from his distressing spirit? *By having David play music.*

6. Who was anointed king before King Saul died? *David.*

7. How did King Saul die? *By falling on his own sword.*

8. Recite I Samuel 16:7.

9. What was David's family line? *Adam, Noah, Shem, Abraham, Judah, Boaz, Obed, Jesse.*

10. Who anointed David king of Israel? *Samuel.*

11. What and who did David kill as a young man? *A lion, a bear, and Goliath.*

12. Why was Saul jealous of David? *The people loved David, and God's Spirit was with him.*

13. What did King Saul try to do to David? *Kill him.*

14. What was David's response to Saul's attempts to kill him? *He fled from Saul but continued to do what was wise and right in the eyes of the Lord.*

15. Recite I Samuel 18:14.

16. How old was David when he became king of Israel? *Thirty.*

17. What city did David conquer which was later called the "City of David"? *Jerusalem.*

18. What did David want to build for God? *The temple.*

19. What sin of David's did we read about in this section? *Numbering the army, trusting in man.*

20. What were the consequences of David's sin*? 70,000 men died.*

21. How did David make preparations for the temple? *By gathering materials.*

SP 140

22. Which son of David's was appointed as king after David? *Solomon.*

23. How long did David reign as king of Israel? *Forty years.*

24. Recite II Samuel 8:15.

25. Who was the third king of Israel? *Solomon.*

26. What did Solomon ask for from God? *Wisdom and knowledge.*

27. What was Israel like when Solomon was king? *United, very large, and prosperous.*

28. What did Solomon write? *3,000 proverbs and 1,005 songs.*

29. What did Solomon build that David was not allowed to build? *The temple.*

30. What was Solomon's sin? *Worshipping false gods, having multiple wives and marrying foreign women.*

31. How long did Solomon rule Israel? *Forty years.*

32. Recite I Kings 11:6.

33. Where was the temple of the Lord built (include city)? *Mt. Moriah, Jerusalem, Israel.*

34. How long did it take to build the temple? *Seven years.*

35. What was the purpose of the temple? *(1) A place for God to dwell among His people and (2) a place of worship and sacrifice for the children of Israel.*

36. Give the size of the temple. *Sixty cubits in length, twenty cubits in width, and thirty cubits in height.*

37. What was in the temple? *The Ark of the Covenant, the altar of incense, the table of showbread, ten menorahs or lampstands.*

38. How was the temple dedicated to God? *With Solomon praying, the people worshipping, and God responding with fire from heaven and His glory filled the temple.*

39. Recite I Kings 6:13.

40. The book of Psalms contains songs written for *worshipping God.*

41. King *David* wrote many of the Psalms.

42. The book of Proverbs is a book of *wise sayings.*

43. King *Solomon* wrote many of the Proverbs.

44. Recite Proverbs 3:5-6.

Section 7 Goals and Key Points

THE PROPHETS

The goal of this lesson is to look briefly at the major and Minor Prophets of the Old Testament.

Key Points:
- Prophets were men sent by God with a message to a king, city, or country.
- God never judged a king, city, or country without first offering the people an opportunity to repent. This offer was usually sent through a prophet.
- There were four Major Prophets: Isaiah, Jeremiah (Lamentations is attributed to Jeremiah), Ezekiel, and Daniel.
- There were twelve Minor Prophets: Hosea, Joel, Amos, Obadiah, Jonah, Micah, Nahum, Habakkuk, Zephaniah, Haggai, Zechariah, and Malachi.

THE KINGS OF ISRAEL

The goal of this lesson is to look at the kings of Israel, how they served, and for how long they reigned.

Key Points:
- God classified kings into two categories: those who did good in His sight and those who did evil in His sight.
- All nineteen kings of Israel did "evil in the eyes of the Lord."

THE DIVIDED KINGDOM: ISRAEL

The goal of this lesson is to examine how Israel became a divided kingdom and the events surrounding the exiling of the people of Israel.

Key Points:
- The kingdom of Israel was divided into two kingdoms during the reign of Rehoboam.
- Israel consisted of ten tribes, and Judah consisted of two tribes.
- Israel sinned by worshipping idols and false gods.
- Israel was taken captive by the Assyrians.
- God promised that He would one day return the people of Israel to their land.

THE KINGS OF JUDAH

The goal of this lesson is to look at the kings of Judah, how they served, and for how long they reigned.

Key Points:
• God classified kings into two categories: those who did good in His sight and those who did evil in His sight.
• Of the twenty kings of Judah, eleven did "evil in the sight of the Lord."
• Of the twenty kings of Judah, seven did "good in the sight of the Lord."
• Two kings of Judah did both good and evil in the sight of the Lord.

THE DIVIDED KINGDOM: JUDAH

The goal of this lesson is to examine how Israel became a divided kingdom and the events surrounding the exiling of the people of Judah.

Key Points:
• The kingdom of Israel was divided into two kingdoms during the reign of Rehoboam.
• Israel consisted of ten tribes, and Judah consisted of two tribes.
• Judah sinned by worshipping idols and false gods.
• Judah was taken captive by the Babylonians.
• God promised that He would one day return the people of Judah to their land.

Level 3

Create a card for Psalms and Proverbs.

- *The book of Psalms is a book of songs written to worship God.*
- *King David wrote many of the psalms.*
- *The book of Proverbs is a book of wise sayings.*
- *King Solomon wrote many of the proverbs.*

Level 4

THE PROPHETS

Topical Bible

Edom was the country to which Obadiah prophesied; who was this area named after?

Nave's, page 130

Bible Dictionary

What is a *prophet*?

Zondervan's, page 476

Concordance

Give the reference for this verse: "Yet the Lord testified against Israel and against Judah, by all of His prophets...."

II Kings 17:13 (Cruden's, page 384)

Quest Question

How does God speak to people today?

Through His Word, the Bible; through people; and through circumstances.

THE PROPHETS

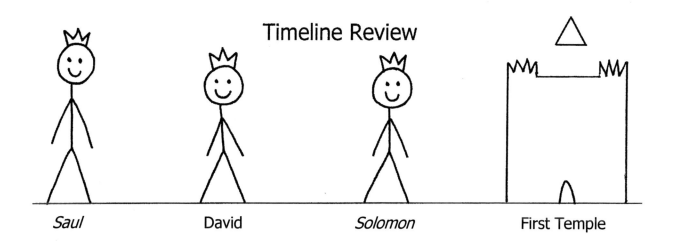

Timeline Review

Saul   David   *Solomon*   First Temple

Bible Verses

Proverbs 3:5-6

I Kings 6:13

I Kings 11:6

THE PROPHETS

Background Bible Reading: The books written by the prophets
Time Frame: From the divided kingdom to the return of the exiles of Judah

A prophet was a man through whom God sent a message for a king, city, or country. *After the kingdom of Israel divided God sent prophets to kings, cities and countries to warn them of coming judgments and encourage them to repent and follow God. God never judged without first offering the people an opportunity to repent.*

I have designed this lesson to begin in the book of Isaiah and go through each book, in order, through Malachi. Students will identify the book, the prophet by the same name, and country to which he prophesied. The only prophet we "skip" will be Daniel, because we will cover his life in the next two lessons. Two of the prophets don't have specific verses referring to whom they prophesied, but I have noted the country in my notes. I have left room after each prophet for your notes.

Isaiah: *Major prophet.*

Draw Isaiah.

Jeremiah: *Major prophet.*

Draw Jeremiah.

Ezekiel: *Major prophet. Please note that the other two "Major Prophet" books are Lamentations and Daniel.*

Draw Ezekiel.

Hosea: *Minor prophet.*

Draw Hosea.

Joel: *Minor prophet.*

Draw Joel.

Amos: *Minor prophet.*

Draw Amos.

THE PROPHETS

Bible Verses: The books written by the prophets
Time Frame: From the divided kingdom to the return of the exiles of Judah

---

| Isaiah 1:1 | A prophet was a man through whom God sent a message for a *king, city,* or *country*. |

| Isaiah 1:1 | Jeremiah 1:1-2 | Ezekiel 1:2 |

Isaiah
Prophesied to: Judah

Jeremiah
Prophesied to: Judah

Ezekiel
Prophesied to: Judah
before and during exile

| Hosea 1:1 | Joel 3:1 | Amos 1:1 |

Hosea
Prophesied to: Judah and Israel

Joel
Prophesied to: Judah

Amos
Prophesied to: Israel

SP 144

THE PROPHETS

Obadiah: *Minor prophet.*

Draw Obadiah.

Jonah: *Minor prophet.*

Draw Jonah.

Micah: *Minor prophet.*

Draw Micah.

Nahum: *Minor prophet.*

Draw Nahum.

Habakkuk: *Habakkuk, a minor prophet, was a prophet to the country of Judah who asked questions of God. God responded by giving him visions which he wrote down and then told to the people of Judah.*

Draw Habakkuk.

Zephaniah: *Minor prophet.*

Draw Zephaniah.

Haggai: *Minor prophet.*

Draw Haggai.

Zechariah: *Minor prophet.*

Draw Zechariah.

Malachi: *Malachi, a minor prophet, was a prophet to the exiles of Judah who returned from Babylon.*

Draw Malachi.

Depending upon your class you, might want to identify the prophet, and then identify on a map the city or country in which he prophesied.

Obadiah 1:1

Obadiah
Prophesied to: Edom

Jonah 1:1-2

Jonah
Prophesied to: Nineveh

Micah 1:1

Micah
Prophesied to: Judah

Nahum 1:1

Nahum
Prophesied to: Nineveh

Habakkuk 1:1-2, 2:2

Habakkuk
Questions/Visions

Zephaniah 1:1

Zephaniah
Prophesied to: Judah

Haggai 1:1

Haggai
Prophesied to: Judah
after the exile

Zechariah 1:1

Zechariah
Prophesied to: Judah
after the exile

Malachi 1:1

Malachi
Prophesied to: Judah
after the exile

Memory Verse: II Kings 17:13

SP 145

Level 3

Create a card for The Prophets

- *A prophet is a man who has a message from God for a king, city or country.*
- *The four Major Prophets are: Isaiah, Jeremiah, Ezekiel, and Daniel.*
- *The twelve Minor Prophets are: Hosea, Joel, Amos, Obadiah, Jonah, Micah, Nahum, Habakkuk, Zephaniah, Haggai, Zechariah, and Malachi.*

Level 4

THE KINGS OF ISRAEL

Topical Bible

What does *Jeroboam's* name mean?

Nave's, page 243.

Bible Dictionary

What did *Jeroboam I* build for Israel at Dan and Bethel?

Zondervan's, page 275.

Concordance

What verse refers to Solomon's effort to kill *Jeroboam*?

I Kings 11:40 (Cruden's page 262)

Quest Question

What effects do the leaders of our country have on the morals of the nation?

Their personal morals affect how well they lead, and others look to them to set moral standards.

SP 146

THE KINGS OF ISRAEL

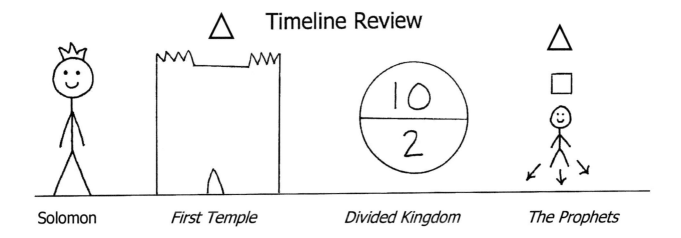

Timeline Review

Solomon   *First Temple*   *Divided Kingdom*   *The Prophets*

Bible Verses

II Kings 17:13

Proverbs 3:5-6

I Kings 6:13

SP 147

THE KINGS OF ISRAEL

Background Bible Reading: I Kings 12-2; II Kings; II Chronicles 10-36
Time Frame: The divided kingdom

Establish for your students the meaning of "did what was right in the sight of the Lord" meant obedience to God's Law; and "did what was evil in the sight of the Lord" meant disobeying God's Law. Israel had nineteen kings who Scripture clearly states "did evil in the sight of the Lord." God judged Israel's sin by sending them into captivity throughout Assyria.

 evil　　　　　　　　*Fill in missing words on the next page.*

The Kings of Israel: *In this section it is important that the students identify each king, note whether he did what was good or evil in the sight of the Lord, and how long that king reigned in Israel.*

Complete the chart on the next page.

THE KINGS OF ISRAEL

Bible Verses: I Kings 14:9-II Kings 17:2
Time Frame: The divided kingdom

A king who did "good" in the sight of the Lord was *obedient* to God's laws.

A king who did "evil" in the sight of the Lord was *disobedient* to God's laws.

King	Reference	Good/Evil	Reign
1. Jeroboam I	I Kings 14: 9-10, 20	*Evil*	*22 years*
2. Nadab	I Kings 15:25-26	*Evil*	*2 years*
3. Baasha	I Kings 15:33-34	*Evil*	*24 years*
4. Elah	I Kings 16:6, 8	*Evil*	*2 years*
5. Zimri	I Kings 16:15, 18-19	*Evil*	*7 days*
6. Omri	I Kings 16:23, 25	*Evil*	*12 years*
7. Ahab	I Kings 16:29-34	*Evil*	*22 years*
8. Ahaziah	I Kings 22:51-53	*Evil*	*2 years*
9. Joram	II Kings 3:1-3	*Evil*	*12 years*
10. Jehu	II Kings 10:28-31	*Evil*	*28 years*
11. Jehoahaz	II Kings 13:1-2	*Evil*	*17 years*

SP 148

THE KINGS OF ISRAEL

1. Who was the first king of Israel after the kingdom divided? *Jeroboam I.*
2. Who was the last king of Israel? *Hosea.*
3. How many kings did Israel have who "did evil in the sight of the Lord"? *Nineteen.*
4. How many kings did Israel have who "did good in the sight of the Lord"? *Zero.*
5. Who was king for the longest time? *Jeroboam II, forty-one years.*
6. Who was king for the shortest time? *Zimri, seven days.*
7. Approximately how many years did Israel's kings reign? *241 years.*
8. What do we learn about God from these kings? *God will allow evil kings to rule over people who have chosen to disobey God's laws. God will also judge the kings and people for their evil actions.*

Complete the chart on the next page.

King	Reference	Good/Evil	Reign
12. Jehoash	II Kings 13:10-11	Evil	16 years
13. Jeroboam II	II Kings 14:23-24	Evil	41 years
14. Zechariah	II Kings 15:8-9	Evil	6 months
15. Shallum	II Kings 15:10, 13-14	Evil	1 month
16. Manahem	II Kings 15:17-18	Evil	10 years
17. Pekahiah	II Kings 15:23-24	Evil	2 years
18. Pekah	II Kings 15:27-28	Evil	20 years
19. Hosea	II Kings 17:1-2	Evil	9 years

Lesson Review

1. Who was the first king of Israel after the kingdom divided?
2. Who was the last king of Israel?
3. How many kings did Israel have who "did evil in the sight of the Lord"?
4. How many kings did Israel have who "did good in the sight of the Lord"?
5. Who was king for the longest time?
6. Who was king for the shortest time?
7. Approximately how many years did Israel's kings reign?
8. What do we learn about God from these kings?

Memory Verse: II Kings 17:18

Level 3

Create a card for the Kings of Israel.

- *Israel had nineteen evil kings.*

Level 4

THE DIVIDED KINGDOM: ISRAEL

Topical Bible

By what other names is the country of *Assyria* known?

Nave's, page 39

Bible Dictionary

What do you learn about the term *captivity* of Israel?

Zondervan's, page 101

Concordance

What is the first mention of *Assyria* in the Bible?

Genesis 2:14 (Cruden's, page 20)

Quest Question

What are some ways that God's people are divided even today?

By worship styles, lifestyles, doctrines, etc.

SP 150

THE DIVIDED KINGDOM: ISRAEL

Timeline Review

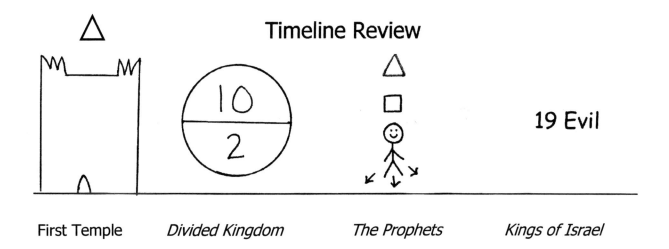

| First Temple | Divided Kingdom | The Prophets | Kings of Israel |

Bible Verses

II Kings 17:18

II Kings 17:13

Proverbs 3:5-6

SP 151

THE DIVIDED KINGDOM: ISRAEL

Background Bible Reading: I Kings 1-22; II Kings; II Chronicles 10-36
Time Frame: The divided kingdom

Divided Kingdom Foretold: *Solomon loved many foreign women and had 700 wives and 300 concubines. As Solomon grew older, he was drawn by his wives to worship false gods. Solomon did what was evil by not following God as David, his father, had done. As a result of Solomon's unfaithfulness God told him that He would tear the kingdom from his son. But because of David's faithfulness, Solomon's son would retain a part of the kingdom.*

 high place   *Draw two men holding a torn sign with the word "kingdom."*

King Solomon's Death: *Solomon had reigned over Israel as king for forty years when he died.*

Draw Solomon's grave.

Israel United—Israel Divided: *Before Solomon's death, the prophet Ahijah went to Jeroboam and told him that God had chosen him to be king over ten of the tribes of Israel. After the death of Solomon, his son Rehoboam became king of all of Israel. Rehoboam was not wise and listened to his friends instead of the elders who had served his father. The people of Israel rebelled against Rehoboam and made Jeroboam king. So the kingdom of Israel divided into two kingdoms, Israel and Judah, as the Lord had promised. Judah consisted of the tribes of Judah and Benjamin and Levites and others from Israel who had a desire to seek the Lord (II Chronicles 11:16-17). Israel consisted of the remaining ten tribes.*

✧ (6) Jerusalem   *Fill in chart on the next page.*

THE DIVIDED KINGDOM: ISRAEL

Bible Verses: I Kings 11:6-17:2
Time Frame: The Divided Kingdom

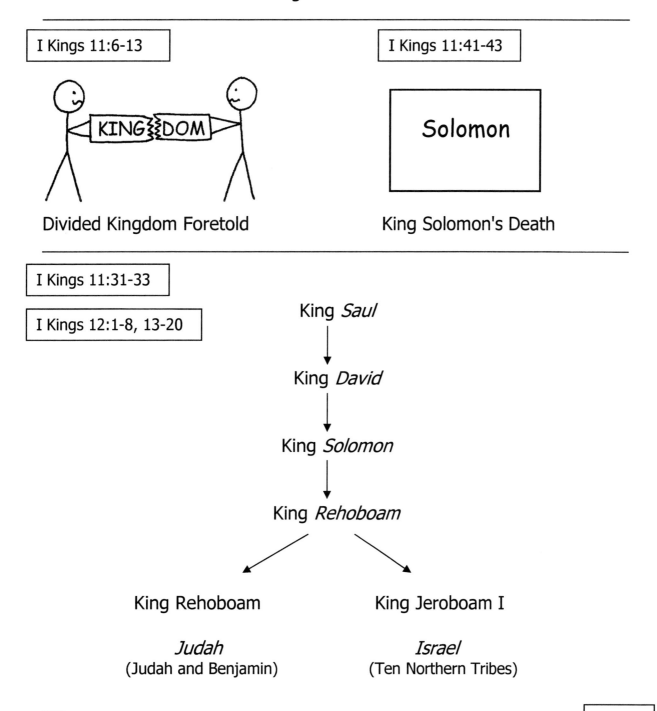

I Kings 11:6-13

Divided Kingdom Foretold

I Kings 11:41-43

Solomon

King Solomon's Death

I Kings 11:31-33

I Kings 12:1-8, 13-20

King *Saul*

↓

King *David*

↓

King *Solomon*

↓

King *Rehoboam*

King Rehoboam

Judah
(Judah and Benjamin)

King Jeroboam I

Israel
(Ten Northern Tribes)

SP 152

THE DIVIDED KINGDOM: ISRAEL

Israel's Sin: *When God first led the Israelites into the Promised Land, God told them to completely remove the people and their idols from the land. Their failure to do this resulted in the children of Israel practicing idolatry and worshipping at high places.*

Draw a man bowing down to an idol.

Israel's Captivity: *The Lord saw that the people still desired to follow after their own sin more than they wanted to follow Him. After many warnings by the prophets, He allowed Assyria to conquer them and take Israel into captivity. I recommend a study of Assyria. The time of Israel's captivity is unknown (indicated by the question marks).*

 (6) Assyrian Empire

 Assyria   *Write Assyria and then draw arrows going out from it and question marks.*

The Promise: *Isaiah promised that God would gather His people from the four corners of the earth where they had been scattered. Ezekiel promised that one day the children of Israel would return to their land, and there they would be His people and He would be their God. Jeremiah promised that one day a return of exiled Israelites would be so great that it would eclipse the Exodus from Egypt.*

Draw Israel and men coming back from four different directions.

1. What did Solomon do that displeased God? *Married many foreign wives who led him into idolatry.*
2. What happened to the kingdom of Israel under King Rehoboam? *It divided into two countries.*
3. What tribes were part of Judah? *Judah and Benjamin.*
4. What tribes were part of Israel? *Reuben, Gad, Manasseh, Simeon, Ephraim, Dan, Naphtali, Asher, Zebulun, Issachar/the ten northern tribes.*
5. Who took Israel captive? *Assyria.*
6. Why was Israel taken captive? *Because of their failure to obey God's commands and their choice to follow after false gods.*
7. How long would Israel's captivity last? *Until God gathers the Israelites from the four corners of the earth and returns them to Israel.*
8. What do we learn about God from these verses? *God keeps His promises but also punishes sin.*

II Kings 17:5-12

II Kings 17:22-23

Israel's Sin

???

Assyria

Israel's Captivity

Isaiah 11:11-12

Ezekiel 36:22-28

Jeremiah 23:3, 7-8

The Promise

Lesson Review

1. What did Solomon do that displeased God?
2. What happened to the kingdom of Israel under King Rehoboam?
3. What tribes were part of Judah?
4. What tribes were part of Israel?
5. Who took Israel captive?
6. Why was Israel taken captive?
7. How long would Israel's captivity last?
8. What do we learn about God from these verses?

Memory Verse: Ezekiel 36:24

SP 153

Level 3

Create a card for The Divided Kingdom Israel.

- *After the death of King Solomon, Israel divided into two countries, Israel and Judah.*
- *The people of Israel sinned against God by worshipping idols at the high places.*
- *God punished Israel by allowing them to be taken captive by the country of Assyria.*
- *God promised Israel that one day He would return them to their land, but the duration of Israel's captivity is unknown.*

Level 4

THE KINGS OF JUDAH

Topical Bible

Give two facts about *Rehoboam* .

Nave's, page 402

Bible Dictionary

What do we learn about the third man named *Manasseh* mentioned in the Bible?

Zondervan's, page 341

Concordance

What are three verses that refer to the *kings of Judah* ?

II Kings 22:18, II Chronicles 35:21, Jeremiah 37:7 (Cruden's, page 272)

Quest Question

What kind of king or leader pleases God?

Those who do things according to God's standards.

SP 154

THE KINGS OF JUDAH

Timeline Review

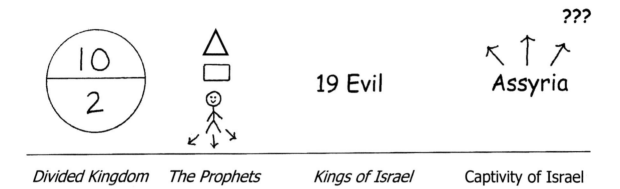

| Divided Kingdom | The Prophets | Kings of Israel | Captivity of Israel |

Bible Verses

Ezekiel 36:24

II Kings 17:18

II Kings 17:13

SP 155

THE KINGS OF JUDAH

Background Bible Reading: I Kings 12-2; II Kings; II Chronicles 10-36
Time Frame: The divided kingdom

---

*Reestablish for your students the meaning of "did what was right in the sight of the Lord"
and "did evil in the sight of the Lord." Judah had eleven kings who Scripture states "did evil
in the sight of the Lord." Judah had seven kings who "did what was good in the sight of the
Lord." God judged Judah's sin by sending them into captivity to Babylon.*

 good   *Fill in missing words on the next page.*

Kings of Judah: *In this section it is important that the students identify each king, noting
whether he did what was good or evil in the sight of the Lord, and how long that king
reigned in Judah.*

THE KINGS OF JUDAH

Bible Verses: I Kings 15:1-II Chronicles 36:14
Time Frame: The divided kingdom

A king who did *good* in the sight of the Lord was obedient to God's laws.

A king who did *evil* in the sight of the Lord was disobedient to God's laws.

King	Reference	Good/Evil	Reign
1. Rehobam	II Chron. 12:1, 13-14	*Evil*	*17 years*
2. Abijah	I Kings 15:1-4	*Evil*	*3 years*
3. Asa	I Kings 15:9-11	*Good*	*41 years*
4. Jehoshaphat	I Kings 22: 41-44	*Good*	*25 years*
5. Jehoram	II Kings 8:16-19	*Evil*	*8 years*
6. Ahaziah	II Kings 8:26-27	*Evil*	*1 year*
7. Athaliah (Queen)	II Chron. 22:10-12	*Evil*	*6 years*
8. Joash	II Chron. 24:1-2, 15-21, 25	*Good/Evil*	*40 years*
9. Amaziah	II Chron. 25:1-2	*Good*	*29 years*
10. Uzziah	II Chron. 26:3-5, 16	*Good*	*52 years*
11. Jotham	II Chron. 27:1-2, 6	*Good*	*16 years*

SP 156

KINGS OF JUDAH

1. Who was the first king of Judah? *Rehoboam.*
2. Who was the last king of Judah? *Zedekiah.*
3. How many kings did Judah have who "did evil in the sight of the Lord"? *Eleven.*
4. How many kings did Judah have who "did good in the sight of the Lord"? *Seven.*
5. How many kings did Judah have who did both evil and good? *Two.*
6. Who was king for the longest time? *Manasseh, fifty-five years.*
7. Who was king for the shortest time? *Jehoahaz and Jehoiachin, three months.*
8. Approximately how many years did Judah's kings reign? *378 years, six months.*
9. What do we learn about God from these kings? *God will allow evil kings to rule a country of people who are also choosing to do evil.*

Complete the chart on the next page.

King	Reference	Good/Evil	Reign
12. Ahaz	II Chron. 28:1-4	*Evil*	*6 years, 5 months*
13. Hezekiah	II Chron. 29:1-2	*Good*	*29 years*
14. Manasseh	II Chron. 33:1-3, 12-16	*Evil/Good*	*55 years*
15. Amon	II Chron. 33:21-24	*Evil*	*2 years*
16. Josiah	II Chron. 34:1-3, 33	*Good*	*31 years*
17. Jehoahaz	II Kings 23:31-32	*Evil*	*3 months*
18. Jehoiakim	II Chron. 36:5	*Evil*	*11 years*
19. Jehoiachin	II Chron. 36:9	*Evil*	*3 months*
20. Zedekiah	II Chron. 36:11-14	*Evil*	*11 years*

Lesson Review

1. Who was the first king of Judah?
2. Who was the last king of Judah?
3. How many kings did Judah have who "did evil in the sight of the Lord"?
4. How many kings did Judah have who "did good in the sight of the Lord"?
5. How many kings did Judah have who did both evil and good?
6. Who was king for the longest time?
7. Who was king for the shortest time?
8. Approximately how many years did Judah's kings reign?
9. What do we learn about God from these kings?

Memory Verse: II Kings 17:19

SP 157

Level 3

Add to the card for the Kings of Judah

- *Judah had eleven evil kings, seven good kings, and two kings who were both good and evil.*

Level 4

THE DIVIDED KINGDOM: JUDAH

Topical Bible

What were some of the symbols that represented *Babylon*?

Nave's, page 46

Bible Dictionary

In what year were the ten Northern tribes (Israel) and Judah taken into *captivity?*

Ten Northern tribes, 722 BC; Judah, 586 BC (Zondervan's, page 101)

Concordance

What is the first mention of the *Babylonians* in Scripture?

Ezekiel 23:15 (Cruden's page 22)

Quest Question

What symbols would represent believers today?

Answers will vary.

SP 158

THE DIVIDED KINGDOM: JUDAH

Timeline Review

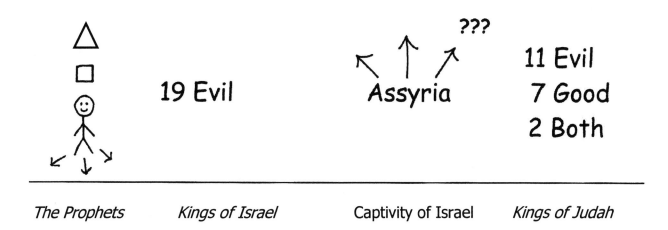

| The Prophets | Kings of Israel | Captivity of Israel | Kings of Judah |

Bible Verses

II Kings 17:19

Ezekiel 36:24

II Kings 17:18

SP 159

THE DIVIDED KINGDOM: JUDAH

Background Bible Reading: I Kings 12-22; II Kings; II Chronicles 10-36
Time Frame: The divided kingdom

Divided Kingdom Foretold: *Reestablish for your students that Solomon loved many foreign women and had 700 wives and 300 concubines. As Solomon grew older he was drawn by his wives into worship of false gods. Solomon had an unfaithful heart toward God, and because of this unfaithfulness, God would take the kingdom away from Solomon and give it to another. However, because of David, the kingdom would be divided after the death of Solomon.*

Draw two men pulling the "kingdom" apart.

King Solomon's Death: *Solomon reigned over Israel as king for forty years and then died.*

Draw the grave of Solomon.

Israel United—Israel Divided: *After the death of Solomon, the kingdom of Israel divided into two separate countries. Judah consisted of the tribes of Judah and Benjamin, and Israel consisted of the remaining ten tribes.*

✧ (6) Jerusalem   *Fill in chart on the next page.*

©2005

THE DIVIDED KINGDOM: JUDAH

Bible Verses: I Kings 11:6-17:2
Time Frame: The Divided Kingdom

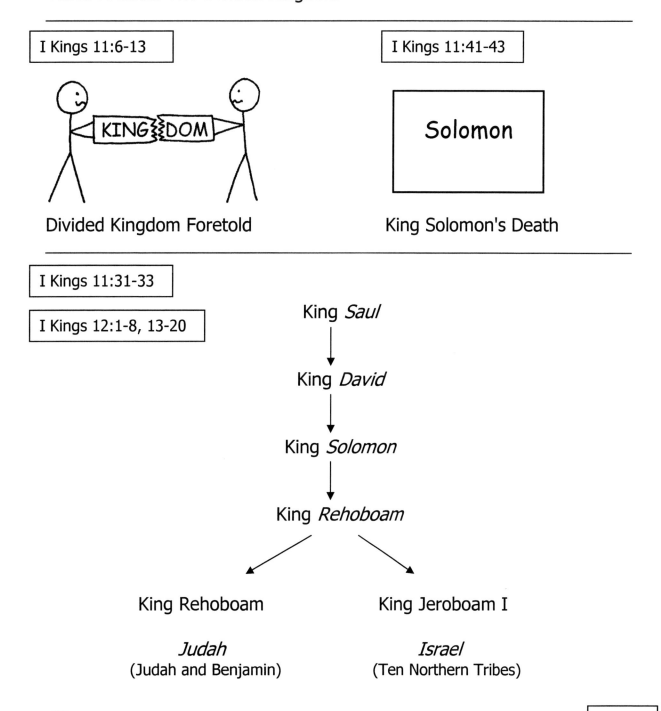

I Kings 11:6-13

Divided Kingdom Foretold

I Kings 11:41-43

Solomon

King Solomon's Death

I Kings 11:31-33

I Kings 12:1-8, 13-20

King *Saul*
↓
King *David*
↓
King *Solomon*
↓
King *Rehoboam*

King Rehoboam

Judah
(Judah and Benjamin)

King Jeroboam I

Israel
(Ten Northern Tribes)

SP 160

THE DIVIDED KINGDOM: JUDAH

Judah's Sin: *Judah failed to follow and obey God's commands and chose instead to follow after other gods.*

Draw a man worshipping at a high place and a broken "commandment" below him.

Judah's Captivity: *Judah was taken captive by the Babylonians in three stages. The first stage was when Daniel was taken; the second stage was when Ezekiel was taken; and the third stage was when the Babylonians conquered Jerusalem and destroyed the temple. The Babylonians then destroyed the temple, plundered the articles from the temple, destroyed the palaces, and took the people captive.*

 (6) Babylonian Empire

Babylon   *Write Babylon and draw three arrows going into it, noting 70 years of captivity.*

The Promise: *The prophet Jeremiah told the people that the captivity of Judah would last seventy years. After seventy years God would bring them back to their own land.*

Write "70 years" and draw arrows leaving "Babylon."

1. What sin did Solomon commit that displeased God? *Idolatry.*
2. What happened to the kingdom of Israel under King Rehoboam? *It divided.*
3. What tribes were part of Judah? *Judah and Benjamin.*
4. What tribes were part of Israel? *Reuben, Gad, Manasseh, Simeon, Ephraim, Dan, Naphtali, Asher, Zebulun, Issachar/ten northern tribes.*
5. Who took Judah captive? *Babylon.*
6. Why was Judah taken captive? *Because they did not follow God's commandments and worshipped false gods/idolatry.*
7. How long would Judah's captivity last? *Seventy years.*
8. What do we learn about God from these verses? *God keeps His promises and punishes sin.*

©2005

II Kings 17:16-19

II Chron. 36:15-20

Jeremiah 25:8-9

70 years

Babylon

Judah's Sin

Judah's Captivity

Jeremiah 25:12

Jeremiah 29:10

70 years later

Babylon

The Promise

Lesson Review

1. What sin did Solomon commit that displeased God?
2. What happened to the kingdom of Israel under King Rehoboam?
3. What tribes were part of Judah?
4. What tribes were part of Israel?
5. Who took Judah captive?
6. Why was Judah taken captive?
7. How long would Judah's captivity last?
8. What do we learn about God from these verses?

Memory Verse: Jeremiah 29:10

SP 161

Review 6

1. What is a prophet? *A man sent by God with a message to a king, city, or country.*

2. Who are the four Major Prophets? *Isaiah, Jeremiah, Ezekiel, and Daniel.*

3. Who are the twelve Minor Prophets? *Hosea, Joel, Amos, Obadiah, Jonah, Micah, Nahum, Habakkuk, Zephaniah, Haggai, Zechariah, and Malachi.*

4. Recite II Kings 17:13

5. What did Solomon do that displeased God? *Married many foreign wives who led him into idolatry.*

6. What happened to the kingdom of Israel under King Rehoboam? *It divided into two countries.*

7. What tribes were part of Judah? *Judah and Benjamin.*

8. What tribes were part of the Israel? *Reuben, Gad, Manasseh, Simeon, Ephraim, Dan, Naphtali, Asher, Zebulun, Issachar/ ten northern tribes.*

9. Who took Israel captive? *Assyria.*

10. Recite II Kings 17:18.

11. Why was Israel taken captive*? Because of their failure to obey God's commands and their choice to follow after false gods.*

12. How long would Israel's captivity last? *Until God gathers the Israelites from the four corners of the earth and returns them to Israel. The time is unknown.*

13. Recite Ezekiel 36:24.

14. How many kings did Judah have who "did evil in the sight of the Lord"? *Eleven.*

SP 162

15. How many kings did Judah have who "did good in the sight of the Lord"? *Seven.*

16. How many kings did Judah have who did both evil and good? *Two.*

17. Recite II Kings 17:19.

18. Who took Judah captive? *Babylon.*

19. Why was Judah taken captive? *Because they did not follow God's commandments and worshipped false gods/idolatry.*

20. How long would Judah's captivity last? *Seventy years.*

21. Recite Jeremiah 29:10.

SP 163

Section 8 Goals and Key Points

DANIEL AND HIS FRIENDS

The goal of this lesson is to look at the early life of Daniel and how, even as a captive, Daniel served the Lord.

Key Points:
- Daniel was taken to Babylon with the first group of captives from Judah.
- Even in captivity, Daniel desired to serve God and follow God's laws.
- God granted Daniel and his friends wisdom and knowledge so that they served as wise men to the king.
- The king had dreams that Daniel was able to interpret which caused the king to acknowledge that the God whom Daniel served was the one true God.

DANIEL AND HIS ENEMIES

The goal of this lesson is to look at one of the events that took place in Daniel's life.

Key Points:
- Daniel was appointed as one of the three governors who served the King of Babylon.
- Because the king favored Daniel for his faithfulness and excellent spirit, Daniel had enemies.
- Daniel's enemies used his commitment to God to try to kill him.
- God miraculously saved Daniel from the lion's den.
- As a result of Daniel's deliverance from the lions, the king worshipped God.

THE SECOND TEMPLE

The goal of this lesson is to look at the events surrounding the return of the first group of exiles from Babylon and their efforts to build the second Temple.

Key Points:
- After the promised seventy years in captivity, God moved on the heart of the king and the exiles of Judah began returning to Jerusalem.
- The first of three groups to return to Jerusalem was led by Zerubbabel.
- The exiles returned with the temple treasures, gold, silver, and animals.
- After returning to Jerusalem, the exiles worshipped and sacrificed to God.
- Even amidst opposition, the temple was completed under the leadership of Zerubbabel and Jeshua.

ESTHER

The goal of this lesson is to look at the life of Esther to see how God protected His people even while they were exiled. The book of Esther takes place between chapters six and seven of the book of Ezra.

Key Points:
- The king of Persia put away his wife and sought a new queen.
- The king chose Esther as the new queen.
- Esther foiled an attempt to have all the Jews in the kingdom killed.
- The Jews established the holiday of Purim to remember this event.

EZRA AND NEHEMIAH

The goal of this lesson is to look at the work of Ezra and Nehemiah in Jerusalem.

Key Points:
- Ezra brought the second group of captives back to Jerusalem.
- Ezra was a teacher of the Law, a priest, and a scribe. He returned to Jerusalem to teach the children of Israel how to live by the Law.
- Nehemiah brought the third group of captives back to Jerusalem to rebuild the walls and gates of Jerusalem.
- The walls and gates of Jerusalem were rebuilt in fifty-two days, despite opposition to the building.
- The events recorded in Nehemiah are the last events, chronologically, of the Old Testament. A 400-year period, often called the "400 Silent Years," followed before the first events of the New Testament began.

Level 3

Create a card for The Divided Kingdom: Judah.

- *After the death of King Solomon, Israel divided into two countries, Israel and Judah.*
- *The people of Judah sinned against God by disobeying the commands of God and by worshipping false gods.*
- *God punished Judah by allowing them to be taken captive by the country of Babylon.*
- *God promised Judah that they would be captive for seventy years, then He would return them to their land.*

Level 4

DANIEL AND HIS FRIENDS

Topical Bible

What does the name *Daniel* mean?

> *Nave's, page 110*

Bible Dictionary

What is the purpose of *visions* in Scripture?

> *Zondervan's, page 601*

Concordance

What is the last time King *Nebuchadnezzar* is mentioned in the Bible?

> *Daniel 5:18. (Cruden's, page 335)*

Quest Question

What are some actions we can take in our day not to "defile" ourselves?

> *Answers will vary. Be careful of what we watch/look at and what we listen to, because these things will effect our beliefs and actions.*

DANIEL AND HIS FRIENDS

Timeline Review

19 Evil	Assyria ???	11 Evil 7 Good 2 Both	Babylon 70 yrs
Kings of Israel	Captivity of Israel	*Kings of Judah*	Captivity of Judah

Bible Verses

Jeremiah 29:10

II Kings 17:19

Ezekiel 36:24

SP 165

DANIEL AND HIS FRIENDS

Background Bible Reading: Daniel 1-5
Time Frame: The beginning of the captivity of Judah

Daniel Was Taken Captive: *The book of Daniel begins with the Babylonians besieging Jerusalem and taking the first of three groups of captives to Babylon. Daniel went with the first group of captives to Babylon, along with the temple treasures/furnishings.*

 (6) Jerusalem

 eunuch   *Draw Daniel and the temple treasures begin taken away.*

Daniel's Heart, God's Favor: *Daniel (Belteshazzar) was taken captive to Babylon with three of his friends, Hananiah (Shadrach), Mishael (Meshach), and Azariah (Abed-Nego). A part of the King's training for these men included special food that was forbidden for Jews by the Law. Daniel appealed to get permission to eat only vegetables and drink only water in order to remain faithful to God's law. After ten days on the diet, Daniel and his friends appeared in better condition than those men on the king's diet. From that point on, Daniel and his friends were allowed to keep their diet.*

Draw Daniel asking for water and vegetables.

Daniel Served the King: *During their captivity, God gave Daniel and his friends knowledge, skill, and wisdom that exceeded the knowledge and the wisdom of the men serving the king. Daniel served King Nebuchadnezzar.*

 visions, dreams, magicians, astrologers   *Draw Daniel and his friends before the king*

DANIEL AND HIS FRIENDS

Bible Verses: Daniel 1:1-5:31
Time Frame: The beginning of the captivity of Judah

Dan. 1:1-4

Daniel Was Taken Captive

Dan. 1:5-16

Dan. 1:17-21

Daniel's Heart, God's Favor

Daniel Served the King

SP 166

DANIEL AND HIS FRIENDS

The King Had a Dream: *King Nebuchadnezzar had a dream that disturbed him greatly. The king ordered that the wise men be brought in to tell him the dream and then give its interpretation. If the wise men were unable to do this for the king, then they would be put to death. When the men came to take Daniel, he asked the king to give him time to interpret the dream; the King granted him his desire.*

 Chaldeans   *Draw the king talking to some of his wise men.*

Daniel Prayed: *Daniel and his friends prayed earnestly for the interpretation of the king's dream. God revealed to Daniel the king's dream and its interpretation.*

 night vision   *Draw Daniel praying.*

Daniel Interpreted the Dream: *Daniel told the king his dream and the interpretation. The king realized that the God whom Daniel served was the true God, and he presented offerings and incense to God.*

Draw Daniel talking to the king.

Daniel was Promoted: *The king promoted Daniel and his friends.*

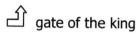 gate of the king   *Draw Daniel being promoted by the king.*

1. When was Daniel taken captive to Babylon? *The beginning of the captivity of Judah.*
2. What, besides people, was taken from Judah to Babylon? *The temple furnishings.*
3. What did Daniel and his friends request regarding food? *That they be given vegetables and water so that they would not defile themselves.*
4. Why were Daniel and his friends chosen to serve the king? *Because God had given them wisdom and knowledge that exceeded the king's other wise men.*
5. What did the king want the wise men of his kingdom to do? *Tell him what he had dreamed and give the interpretation of the dream.*
6. What did Daniel do when he found out about the dream? *He asked the king to give him time to pray and ask God for the interpretation.*
7. What happened as a result of Daniel being able to tell the king his dream and its interpretation? *He and his friends were promoted.*
8. What do we learn about God from these verses? *Even in situations where there is great pressure and great danger around God's people, He takes care of them.*

Dan. 2:1-16

The King Had a Dream

Dan. 2:17-23

Daniel Prayed

Dan. 2:24-28, 46-47

Daniel Interpreted the Dream

Dan. 2:48-49

Daniel was Promoted

Lesson Review

1. When was Daniel taken captive to Babylon?
2. What, besides people, was taken from Judah to Babylon?
3. What did Daniel and his friends request regarding food?
4. Why were Daniel and his friends chosen to serve the king?
5. What did the king want the wise men of his kingdom to do?
6. What did Daniel do when he found out about the dream?
7. What happened as a result of Daniel being able to tell the king his dream and its interpretation?
8. What do we learn about God from these verses?

Memory Verse: Daniel 1:8

SP 167

Level 3

Create a card for Daniel.

- *Daniel was taken as a captive from Judah to Babylon when he was a young man.*
- *The king of Babylon promoted Daniel after he interpreted the king's dream.*

Level 4

DANIEL AND HIS ENEMIES

Topical Bible

What is a *decree*?

Nave's, page 117

Bible Dictionary

What was a *governor*?

Zondervan's, page 205

Concordance

What passages in Daniel have the word *sealed* in them?

Daniel 6:17, 12:9 (Cruden's, page 427)

Quest Question

What should be our response when we are threatened physically because of our faith?

Answers will vary, but we should strive to emulate Daniel and pray.

SP 168

DANIEL AND HIS ENEMIES

Timeline Review

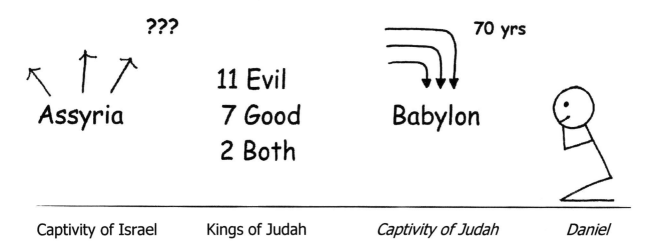

Captivity of Israel	Kings of Judah	*Captivity of Judah*	*Daniel*

Bible Verses

Daniel 1:8

Jeremiah 29:10

II Kings 17:19

SP 169

DANIEL AND HIS ENEMIES

Background Bible Reading: Daniel 6
Time Frame: During the captivity of Judah in Babylon

Daniel's Position: *King Darius set over his kingdom three governors and under them 120 satraps so that no loss would be suffered by the king. Daniel was appointed as one of the three governors.*

 governors, satraps   *Draw the king, three governors and satraps.*

Daniel's Enemies: *Because of Daniel's excellent spirit and faithfulness, the king considered putting Daniel over the whole realm. This caused the other governors and some of the satraps to become his enemies. These enemies then wanted to discredit him, but the only way they could do that was to use his service to God as the means to destroy him.*

Draw the king thinking about Daniel and the other governors plotting.

The Evil Plan: *Daniel's enemies persuaded the king to issue a decree that anyone who was found worshipping any god or man but the king, would be thrown to the lions.*

Draw two governors with a scroll.

Daniel's Response: *When Daniel heard that the decree had been signed, the first thing he did was go home and pray like he had done every day before.*

 decree

©2005

Draw Daniel praying.

DANIEL AND HIS ENEMIES

Bible Verses: Daniel 6
Time Frame: During the captivity of Judah in Babylon

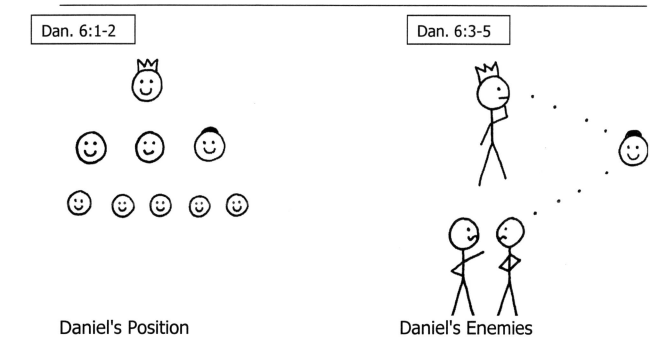

Dan. 6:1-2	Dan. 6:3-5
Daniel's Position	Daniel's Enemies

Dan. 6:6-9

Dan. 6:10

The Evil Plan

Daniel's Response

SP 170

DANIEL AND HIS ENEMIES

Daniel Was Found Praying: *Daniel's enemies gathered and found him praying and then accused Daniel before the king. Although the king liked Daniel, he was unable to reverse the sentence against Daniel.*

Draw Daniel in chains before the king and two governors.

Daniel Was Thrown to the Lions: *Before sealing the den of the lions, the king stated that Daniel's God would deliver him. Then Daniel was thrown into the den of lions, a large stone was rolled over the den, and the stone was sealed.*

Draw Daniel being thrown into the lions' den.

God Protected Daniel: *The king was very disturbed about putting Daniel in the lions' den and spent the night fasting and awake. Early the next morning he went to the den and called down to Daniel, who answered him. Daniel stated that an angel had shut the mouths of the lions because he was an innocent man. The king then had Daniel removed from the lions' den.*

Draw Daniel in the lions' den with lions' mouths closed.

Daniel's God Was Proclaimed: *After Daniel was removed from the lions' den, the king had Daniel's enemies, who had accused him unjustly, thrown into the lions' den, where they died immediately. King Darius then praised God and commanded that throughout his kingdom the God whom Daniel worshipped should be feared.*

Draw the enemies of Daniel being thrown into the lions' den.

---

1. What was Daniel's position under King Darius? *One of three governors.*
2. Why did Daniel's enemies want to get rid of him? *He was favored by King Darius.*
3. What was the plan to kill Daniel? *To have the king issue a decree that anyone found worshipping any man or god but the king would be thrown into the lions' den.*
4. What was Daniel's response when he learned of the decree to worship no god but the king? *Daniel prayed as he usually did.*
5. When Daniel was found praying, what happened to him? *He was taken to the king and thrown into the lions' den.*
6. What happened to Daniel in the lions' den? *An angel of God protected him, and he was not harmed in any way.*
7. What happened to Daniel's enemies? *His enemies, along with their families, were thrown to the lions and died.*
8. What was the response of the king when Daniel was not killed? *He praised God.*
9. What do we learn about God from these verses? *God can protect the innocent. God wants us to trust Him and worship only Him, even if it costs us our lives.*

Dan. 6: 11-14

Daniel Was Found Praying

Dan. 6:15-17

Daniel Was Thrown to the Lions

Dan. 6:18-23

God Protected Daniel

Daniel 6:24-28

Daniel's God Was Proclaimed

Lesson Review

1. What was Daniel's position under King Darius?
2. Why did Daniel's enemies want to get rid of him?
3. What was the plan to kill Daniel?
4. What was Daniel's response when he learned of the decree to worship no god but the king?
5. When Daniel was found praying, what happened to him?
6. What happened to Daniel in the lions' den?
7. What happened to Daniel's enemies?
8. What was the response of the king when Daniel was not killed?
9. What do we learn about God from these verses?

Memory Verse: Daniel 6:10

SP 171

Level 3

Add to the card for Daniel

- *Daniel served four different kings in Babylon.*
- *Daniel was thrown into the lions' den because he prayed to his God.*
- *God protected Daniel in the lions' den.*
- *The king worshipped God after seeing God protect Daniel in the lions' den.*

Level 4

THE SECOND TEMPLE

Topical Bible

What does *exile* refer to?

Nave's, page 145

Bible Dictionary

What does the name *Zerubbabel* mean?

Zondervan's, page 617

Concordance

In what books of the Bible is King *Cyrus* mentioned?

II Chronicles, Ezra, Isaiah, and Daniel (Cruden's, page 99)

Quest Question

Only a small percentage of the Jews living in Babylon returned to Jerusalem with Zerubbabel. Why do you think this was?

They didn't know the promise; they liked their jobs; they were happy where they were; etc.

SP 172

THE SECOND TEMPLE

Timeline Review

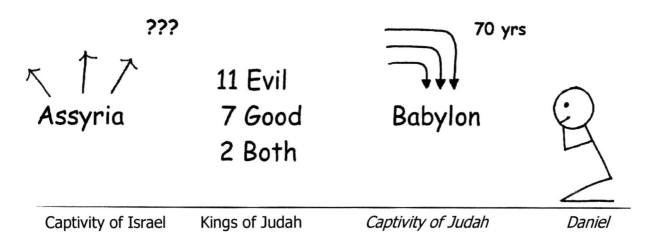

Captivity of Israel   Kings of Judah   *Captivity of Judah*   *Daniel*

Bible Verses

Daniel 6:10

Daniel 1:8

Jeremiah 29:10

SP 173

THE SECOND TEMPLE

Background Bible Reading: Ezra 1-6
Time Frame: After the first group of captives returned from Babylon

---

King Cyrus' Proclamation: *God fulfilled His promise to Judah to return them to their land after seventy years in captivity to Babylon. In the first year of King Cyrus's reign in Persia, the king made a proclamation that those who were in his kingdom that were taken captive from Judah could return. The captives were to return and rebuild the temple of God in Jerusalem. This temple is important because it is the temple in which Jesus, the Messiah, would worship. The men of Persia were commanded to give the returning captives gifts of silver, gold, goods, and livestock to be used as a freewill offering to God.*

 freewill offering   *Draw King Cyrus making a decree.*

The First Exiles Returned: *The exiles included the heads of the families of Benjamin and Judah, the priests, Levites, and all those on whom the Spirit of God moved to return to Jerusalem.*

 (6) Jerusalem   *See list of returning exiles on the next page.*

Cyrus Returned the Temple Treasures: *King Cyrus also sent the temple treasures taken by Nebuchadnezzar back with those returning to Jerusalem.*

Draw the temple treasures and the people returning.

People and Animals Returned: *The total number of captives that returned was 49,897. The animals included 736 horses, 245 mules, 435 camels, and 6,720 donkeys.*

See notes on the next page.

THE SECOND TEMPLE

Bible Verses: Ezra 1:1-6:16
Time Frame: After the first group captives returned from Babylon

---

Ezra 1:1-4

King Cyrus' Proclamation

Ezra 1:5

Levites

Priests

Leaders of the tribe of Judah

Leaders of the tribe of to
 Benjamin

Those Jews wanting to return
 to Israel

The First Exiles Returned

Ezra 1:7-11

Cyrus Returned the Temple Treasures

Ezra 2:1, 64-67

 48,897 people

 736 horses

 245 mules

435 camels

 6,720 donkeys

People and Animals Returned

SP 174

THE SECOND TEMPLE

Worship Was Restored to Jerusalem: *Seven months after returning from captivity, the children of Israel gathered in Jerusalem, where the priests built an altar and re-established the routine temple offerings and sacrifices.*

 burnt offering, Feast of Tabernacles   *Draw the people worshipping in Jerusalem.*

The Building of the Second Temple: *In the second month of the second year, the rebuilding of the temple began under the leadership of Zerubbabel and Jeshua. When the foundation for the temple was laid, the priests and Levites praised God.*

Draw people rebuilding the temple.

The Resistance: *Some of the enemies of the people of Judah came to them requesting that they be allowed to help rebuild the temple. Zerubabbel and the leaders told them that they would not allow them to help. As a result the enemies tried to discourage the people and hired counselors in an attempt to frustrate and stall the progress of the building.*

 adversaries   *Draw one man building and one man holding a scroll.*

The Temple Was Completed: *The completion of the temple came in the sixth year of King Darius of Persia. A great celebration followed the dedication of the temple.*

Draw the completed temple and a priest worshipping.

---

1. What king of Persia sent the captives from Babylon back from Judah? *Cyrus.*
2. What did the king want them to do when they returned to Jerusalem? *Rebuild the temple.*
3. Who was included in the first group of exiles to return? *Leaders of the tribes of Benjamin and Judah, priests, Levites, and those whom God's Spirit moved to return.*
4. What did the children of Israel take with them back to Israel? *The temple treasures, silver, gold, goods, and livestock.*
5. What happened in the second month after the exiles returned? *The children of Israel gathered in Jerusalem, built an altar, and worshipped the Lord.*
6. What did the priests and Levites do when the foundation of the temple was laid? *Praised God.*
7. Who resisted the rebuilding of the temple? *The enemies of the children of Israel.*
8. Who was king of Persia when the temple was finished? *Darius.*
9. What do we learn about God from these verses? *God is faithful to His promises and His people. God also intends for His people to have a place of worship.*

Ezra 3:1-6

Ezra 3:8-10

Worship Was Restored to Jerusalem   The Building of the Second Temple

___

Ezra 4:1-5

Ezra 6:15-16

The Resistance   The Temple Was Completed

___

Lesson Review

1. What king of Persia sent the captives from Babylon back from Judah?
2. What did the king want them to do when they returned to Jerusalem?
3. Who was included in the first group of exiles to return?
4. What did the children of Israel take with them back to Israel?
5. What happened in the second month after the exiles returned?
6. What did the priests and Levites do when the foundation of the temple was laid?
7. Who resisted the rebuilding of the temple?
8. Who was king of Persia when the temple was finished?
9. What do we learn about God from these verses?

Memory Verse: Ezra 6:16

SP 175

©2005

Level 3

Create a card for The Second Temple.

- *The second temple was built under the leadership of Zerubbabel and Jeshua.*
- *The second temple was built after King Cyrus (of Babylon) sent the first captives of Judah back.*
- *The first group of captives returned with the temple treasures, precious metals and animals.*
- *Seven months after the exiles returned they gathered in Jerusalem to worship God.*

Level 4

ESTHER

Topical Bible

What was another name for *Esther*?

> *Nave's, page 142*

Bible Dictionary

What does *Vashti* mean?

> *Zondervan's, page 599*

Concordance

If you were doing research on *Purim*, where would you begin?

> *Esther 9:26 (Cruden's, page 387)*

Quest Question

What holidays do we currently celebrate that are a remembrance of God's works?

> *Easter, Christmas, Independence Day, etc.*

ESTHER

Timeline Review

11 Evil
7 Good
2 Both

70 yrs

Babylon

Kings of Judah   *Captivity of Judah*   *Daniel*   *The Second Temple*

Bible Verses

Ezra 6:16

Daniel 6:10

Daniel 1:8

SP 177

ESTHER

Background Bible Reading: The Book of Esther
Time Frame: During the Captivity of Israel

The story of Esther takes place between chapters six and seven of the book of Ezra.

The King Banished the Queen: *King Ahasuerus held a feast, and at the end, he called for the queen to show her off, but she refused to go to him.*

 (7) Persian Empire   *Draw the king banishing queen Vashti.*

The Search for a New Queen: *Because of queen Vashti's actions the wise men of the kingdom counseled the king to banish her. When the king regretted banishing queen Vashti, the wise men recommended that he choose a new queen.*

Draw a man reading from a scroll.

Esther Was Taken to the Palace: *Esther was chosen as one of the young women who would be considered for queen. Esther's cousin, Mordecai, told her not to reveal her Jewish background when she went to the palace. At the palace, Esther found favor with the custodian of the women and received special treatment.*

 (7) Susa/Shushan

 citadel   *Draw Esther going to the palace.*

Esther Was Chosen as Queen: *After one year of beauty treatments, Esther was summoned by the king. The king loved Esther so much that she became his new queen.*

Draw the king crowning Esther as queen.

ESTHER

Bible Verses: The Book of Esther
Time Frame: During the Captivity of Israel

Esther 1:1-4, 10-12, 19

The King Banished the Queen

Esther 2:1-4

The Search for a New Queen

Esther 2:5-10

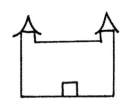

Esther Was Taken to the Palace

Esther 2:15-18

Esther Chosen as Queen

SP 178

ESTHER

Haman's Plot to Kill the Jews: *Haman's new position required that people bow down to him to honor him. However, Mordecai would not bow to Haman. Haman was filled with wrath and sought to destroy not just Mordecai, but all of Mordecai's people living in the kingdom. Haman convinced the king to allow him to do this. The decree was sent and the date set for the elimination of the Jews.*

 homage

Draw Haman showing a scroll to the king.

Mordecai Told Esther the Plot: *Mordecai learned of Haman's plot to kill all the Jews in the kingdom and told Esther about it. Mordecai also reminded her that God could use her, as queen, to help save her people. Esther requested that the Jews of the kingdom join her in fasting and praying before she went to the king.*

Draw Mordecai talking to Esther.

Haman's Plot Ended: *Risking her life, Esther appeared before the king, who spared her life, and invited him and Haman to a banquet. At the banquet Esther exposed Haman's plot and pleaded for her life and the lives of the other Jews in the kingdom. The king was so upset that he ordered Haman to be hanged on the very gallows he had erected for killing Mordecai.*

Draw the king, and Esther pointing to Haman.

The Jews Were Saved: *Although the king could not revoke his law regarding the Jews, he did issue a decree that the Jews could defend themselves. In the battles that day, the Jews prevailed. Because of Esther's position and her great courage, the Jews were saved. The holiday of Purim was established to remember this event.*

Purim

Draw the queen, the king, and Mordecai.

1. Why was the king searching for a new queen? *Because Queen Vashti had disobeyed him and he had banished her.*
2. What did Mordecai tell Esther not to reveal when she went to the palace? *Her Jewish heritage.*
3. For what position did the king select Esther? *Queen.*
4. Why did Haman want to kill the Jews? *Because Mordecai would not bow down to him.*
5. What happened when Mordecai found out about Haman's evil plot? *He told Esther of Haman's plot and told her to go to the king and plead for the lives of the Jews.*
6. How did Esther save her fellow Jews? *By revealing Haman's plot to kill Jews to the king.*
7. What happened to Haman? *He was killed on the gallows that he had built.*
8. What happened to the Jews in that country? *They were told that they could defend themselves, and as a result they were not killed.*
9. What do we learn about God from these verses? *God puts His people in various places so that they can help and protect His people.*

©2005

Esther 3:1-6, 8-11, 13

Esther 4:1, 6-17

Haman's Plot to Kill the Jews

Mordecai Told Esther the Plot

Esther 5:1-5; 7:1-10

Esther 9:1-3, 27-28

Haman's Plot Ended

The Jews were Saved

Lesson Review

1. Why was the king searching for a new queen?
2. What did Mordecai tell Esther not to reveal when she went to the palace?
3. Of what position did the king select Esther?
4. Why did Haman want to kill the Jews?
5. What happened when Mordecai found out about Haman's evil plot?
6. How did Esther save her fellow Jews?
7. What happened to Haman?
8. What happened to the Jews in that country?
9. What do we learn about God from these verses?

Memory Verse: Esther 4:14

©2005

SP 179

Level 3

Create a card for Esther.

- *Esther, a Jewish woman, was chosen to be queen of Persia.*
- *Esther called her people to prayer and fasting when she learned that there was a plot to kill the Jewish people in Persia.*
- *After exposing the plot to kill the Jews to the king, the king enabled the Jews to defend themselves.*
- *The holiday of Purim was established to remember how God delivered the Jews using Esther.*

Level 4

EZRA AND NEHEMIAH

Topical Bible

Who was *Ezra* ?

Nave's, page 147

Bible Dictionary

What does *Nehemiah* mean?

Zondervan's, page 394

Concordance

How often are *scribes* mentioned in the Old Testament?

5 times (Cruden's, page 425)

Quest Question

At the end of the Old Testament there is still the promise of God that He will return His people to their land. Could we be seeing this even in our time?

I recommend teachers do research to see what is currently happening in Israel, especially in the area of immigration.

©2005

SP 180

EZRA AND NEHEMIAH

Timeline Review

| Captivity of Judah | *Daniel* | The Second Temple | *Esther* |

Bible Verses

Esther 4:14

Ezra 6:16

Daniel 6:10

SP 181

EZRA AND NEHEMIAH

Background Bible Reading: The Books of Ezra and Nehemiah
Time Frame: At the end of the captivity of Judah

Ezra and the Second Group of Exiles: *The king of Persia, Artaxerxes, granted Ezra's request to return to Israel. Ezra returned with some of the children of Israel, priests, Levites, and other temple servants.*

Draw Ezra and a group of people returning to Israel.

Ezra, the Priest and Teacher: *God was with Ezra, and Ezra had prepared his heart to seek the Law of God and to teach others how to live a holy life to please God. Ezra was a priest, a scribe, and a teacher of the Law.*

Draw Ezra and note his positions.

Nehemiah Prayed: *Nehemiah received word from Judah that the walls and gates around Jerusalem were broken and burned down. This caused Nehemiah to fast and pray.*

Draw Nehemiah praying.

Nehemiah's Request: *After praying, Nehemiah (the king's cup bearer) was asked by the king what was troubling him and what was his request of the king. Before answering, Nehemiah prayed, and then requested that he be allowed to return to Jerusalem to help rebuild the walls and gates of the city. The king granted Nehemiah's request and gave him territorial passes and timber for the rebuilding project.*

cup bearer

Draw Nehemiah talking to the king

EZRA AND NEHEMIAH

Bible Verses: The Books of Ezra and Nehemiah
Time Frame: At the end of the captivity of Judah

Ezra 7:1, 6-8

Ezra and the Second Group of Exiles

Ezra 7:9-11

Priest
Scribe
Teacher

Ezra, the Priest and Teacher

Neh. 1:1-4, 11

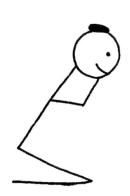

Nehemiah Prayed

Neh. 2:1-8

Nehemiah's Request

SP 182

EZRA AND NEHEMIAH

Nehemiah and the Walls: *Nehemiah returned to Jerusalem with the third group of exiles. After arriving, Nehemiah went by night and surveyed the condition of Jerusalem's walls and gates. After seeing the walls, Nehemiah encouraged the people to rebuild the walls, and they agreed to do it.*

(7) Jerusalem

gates, walls   *Draw Nehemiah talking to the people with the wall partly built.*

The Opposition: *As Nehemiah and the people began rebuilding the walls and gates, they had opposition from some of the local leaders who did not want to see the walls and gates rebuilt. Amidst the opposition, the people prayed and, holding a weapon with one hand, they continued building with the other.*

Draw a man building and one man with a scroll.

The Wall and Gates Were Finished: *Fifty-two days after starting the rebuilding of the walls and gates of Jerusalem the people, under Nehemiah's leadership, completed the project.*

Draw the gates of Jerusalem.

Ezra Read the Law: *The people gathered together in Jerusalem, where Ezra read the Law to them and God gave them understanding. Nehemiah served as governor, Ezra served as the priest and scribe, and the Levites taught the people the Law. With these events the chronological events of the Old Testament come to a close. The following 400 years are known as the "400 Silent Years," because no Scripture was given during that time.*

Draw Ezra reading the Law to the people.

1. Who led the second group of captives back from Babylon to Jerusalem? *Ezra.*
2. What positions did Ezra hold? *Priest, scribe, and teacher of the Law.*
3. Why did Nehemiah pray? *Because the walls/gates of Jerusalem were broken/burned.*
4. What did Nehemiah request of the king? *That he be allowed to return to Jerusalem to rebuild the walls and gates of Jerusalem.*
5. Who led the third group of captives back from Babylon to Jerusalem? *Nehemiah.*
6. What did the people and Nehemiah rebuild? *The walls and gates of Jerusalem.*
7. How long did it take to complete the building of the walls? *Fifty-two days.*
8. When Ezra read the Law, how did the people respond? *By worshiping and weeping.*
9. What do we learn about God from these verses? *God kept His promise to Judah, and they returned, as promised, to Jerusalem. We can look forward to seeing God fulfill His promise to Israel and their return from exile.*

Neh. 2:11-18

Neh. 4:1-3, 6-9, 16-17

Nehemiah and the Walls

The Opposition

Neh. 6:15-16

Neh. 8:1-3, 6-9

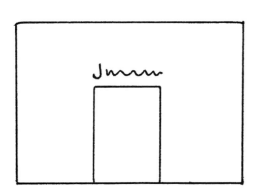

The Wall and Gates Were Finished

Ezra Read the Law

Lesson Review

1. Who led the second group of captives back from Babylon to Jerusalem?
2. What positions did Ezra hold?
3. Why did Nehemiah pray?
4. What did Nehemiah request of the king?
5. Who led the third group of captives back from Babylon to Jerusalem?
6. What did the people and Nehemiah rebuild?
7. How long did it take to complete the building of the walls?
8. When Ezra read the Law, how did the people respond?
9. What do we learn about God from these verses?

Memory Verse: Nehemiah 1:9

SP 183

EZRA AND NEHEMIAH

Character/Event Cards

Create a card for Ezra and Nehemiah.

- *Ezra brought the second group of captives back to Jerusalem.*
- *Ezra was a teacher of the Law, a priest, and a scribe. He returned to Jerusalem to teach the children of Israel how to live by the Law.*
- *Nehemiah brought the third group of captives back to Jerusalem to rebuild the walls and gates of Jerusalem.*
- *The events recorded in Nehemiah are the last events, chronologically of the Old Testament.*

Ezra and Nehemiah

Write your memory verse:

Nehemiah 1:9

SP 184

Review 7

1. When was Daniel taken captive to Babylon? *The beginning of the captivity of Judah.*

2. What, besides people, was taken from Judah to Babylon? *The temple furnishings, gold, silver, and livestock.*

3. What did Daniel and his friends request regarding food? *That they be given vegetables and water so that they would not defile themselves.*

4. Why were Daniel and his friends chosen to serve the king? *Because God had given them wisdom and knowledge that exceeded the king's wise men.*

5. What did the king want the wise men of his kingdom to do? *Tell him what he had dreamed and give the interpretation of the dream.*

6. What did Daniel do when he found out about the king's dream? *He asked the king to give him time to pray and ask God for the interpretation.*

7. What happened as a result of Daniel being able to tell the king his dream and its interpretation? *He and his friends were promoted.*

8. Recite Daniel 1:8.

9. Why did Daniel's enemies want to get rid of him? *He was favored by king Darius.*

10. What was the plan to kill Daniel? *To have the king issue a decree that anyone found worshipping any man/god but the king would be thrown into the lion's den.*

11. What was Daniel's response when he learned of the decree to worship no god but the king? *Daniel prayed, as he usually did.*

12. When Daniel was found praying, what happened to him? *He was taken to the king and thrown into the lions' den.*

13. What happened to Daniel in the lions' den? *An angel of God protected him, and he was not harmed in any way.*

14. What happened to Daniel's enemies? *His enemies, along with their families, were thrown to the lions' and died.*

15. What was the response of the king when Daniel was not killed? *He praised God.*

16. Recite Daniel 6:10.

17. What king of Persia sent the captives from Babylon back to Judah? *Cyrus.*

18. What did the king want them to do when they returned to Jerusalem? *Rebuild the temple.*

19. Who was included in the first group of exiles to return? *Leaders of the tribes of Benjamin and Judah, priests, Levites, and those whom God's Spirit moved to return.*

SP 184-185

20. What did the children of Israel take with them back to Israel? *The temple treasures, silver, gold, goods, and livestock.*

21. What happened in the second month after the exiles returned? *The children of Israel gathered in Jerusalem, built an altar, and worshipped the Lord.*

22. What did the priests and Levites do when the foundation of the temple was laid? *They praised God.*

23. Who resisted the rebuilding of the temple? *The enemies of the children of Israel.*

24. Who was king of Persia when the temple was finished? *Darius.*

25. Recite Ezra 6:16.

26. Why was the king searching for a new queen? *Because Queen Vashti had disobeyed him and he had banished her.*

27. What did Mordecai tell Esther not to reveal when she went to the palace? *Her Jewish heritage.*

28. For what position did the king select Esther? *Queen.*

29. Why did Haman want to kill the Jews? *Because Mordecai would not bow down to him.*

30. What happened when Mordecai found out about Haman's evil plot? *He told Esther of Haman's plot and told her to go to the king and plead for the lives of the Jews.*

31. How did Esther save her fellow Jews? *By revealing Haman's plot to kill Jews to the king.*

32. What happened to Haman? *He was killed on the gallows that he had built.*

33. What happened to the Jews in that country? *They were told that they could defend themselves, and as a result they were not killed.*

34. Recite Esther 4:14.

35. Who led the second group of captives back from Babylon to Jerusalem? *Ezra.*

36. What positions did Ezra hold? *Priest, scribe, and teacher of the Law.*

37. Why did Nehemiah pray? *Because the walls/gates of Jerusalem were broken/burned.*

38. What did Nehemiah request of the king? *That he be allowed to return to Jerusalem to rebuild the walls and gates of Jerusalem.*

39. Who led the third group of captives back from Babylon to Jerusalem? *Nehemiah.*

40. What did the people and Nehemiah rebuild? *The walls and gates of Jerusalem.*

41. How long did it take to complete the building of the walls? *Fifty-two days.*

42. When Ezra read the Law, how did the people respond? *By worshiping and weeping.*

43. Recite Nehemiah 1:9.

44. As we complete the Old Testament Overview, what are some of the things we know about the coming Messiah from the Old Testament? *Messiah would be born of woman, born of the line of Abraham, and born of the line of David.*

©2005

SP 186-185

The Old Testament Timeline

Final Review

Old Testament Timeline

Creation
1
2
3
4
5
6
7 days

God

Genesis

Adam and Eve

The Fall

Sin → Death

Punished/Promised/Provided

Noah

The Flood

Grapevine Studies
Old Testament

Old Testament Timeline

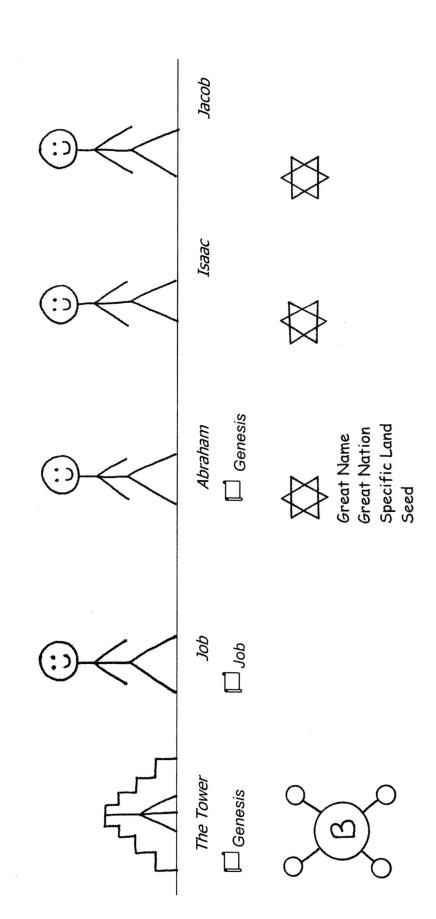

The Tower

□ Genesis

Job

□ Job

Abraham

□ Genesis

Great Name
Great Nation
Specific Land
Seed

Isaac

Jacob

Old Testament Timeline

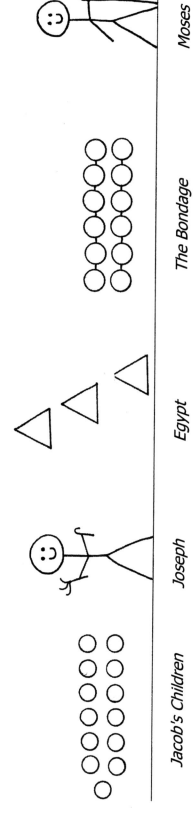

Jacob's Children

Joseph

Egypt

The Bondage

Moses

☐ Genesis

☐ Exodus

282

Old Testament Timeline

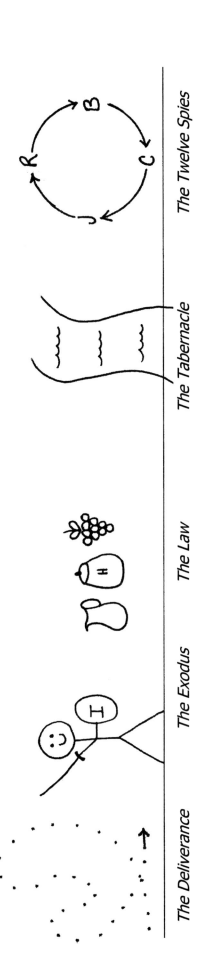

The Deliverance · The Exodus · The Law · The Tabernacle · The Twelve Spies

Exodus

Leviticus, Numbers, Deuteronomy

283

Old Testament Timeline

The Desert   Joshua   The Promised Land   The Jordan   The Judges

B

C

R

J

☐ Joshua

☐ Judges

Old Testament Timeline

Ruth Samuel Saul David Solomon

☐ Ruth

☐ Samuel

☐ II Samuel

☐ I Chronicles

☐ Psalms

☐ Chronicles and I Kings

☐ Proverbs, Ecclesiastes
    Song of Solomon

SP 193-192

Old Testament Timeline

First Temple

The Divided Kingdom

The Prophets

19 Evil

Kings of Israel

Israel's Captivity

Israel

Judah

10

2

Assyria

???

☐ I-II Kings, II Chronicles

Prophet to both Israel and Judah
☐ Hosea

Prophets to Nineveh
☐ Jonah
   Nahum

Prophet to Edom
☐ Obadiah

☐ I-II Kings and II Chronicles

Prophet to Israel
☐ Amos

286

Old Testament Timeline

70 Years
Babylon

11 Evil
7 Good
2 Both

| Kings of Judah | Judah's Captivity | Daniel | Second Temple |

Prophets to Judah
Isaiah
Jeremiah
Ezekiel
Joel
Micah
Habakkuk
Zephaniah
Haggai
Zechariah
Malachi

I-II Kings and II Chronicles

Lamentations

Daniel

Ezra

SP 195-194

Old Testament Timeline

O.T. | N.T.

400 Years

400 Silent Years

Esther

Ezra

Nehemiah

☐ Esther

☐ Ezra

☐ Ezra and Nehemiah

SP 196-195

288

Final Review

Recite or write the following verses on a separate sheet of paper.

1. Genesis 1:1
2. Genesis 1:31
3. Genesis 2:7
4. Genesis 3:15
5. Genesis 6:8
6. Genesis 11:9
7. Job 1:22
8. Genesis 22:18
9. Genesis 26:4
10. Genesis 35:12
11. Genesis 39:2
12. Genesis 50:24
13. Exodus 2:24
14. Exodus 10:2
15. Exodus 15:19
16. Deuteronomy 6:5
17. Exodus 29:45
18. Deuteronomy 8:2
19. Deuteronomy 1:8
20. Joshua 4:23

21. Judges 21:25
22. Ruth 1:16
23. I Samuel 3:19
24. I Samuel 16:7
25. I Samuel 18:14
26. II Samuel 8:15
27. I Kings 11:6
28. I Kings 6:13
29. Proverbs 3:5-6
30. II Kings 17:13
31. II Kings 17:18
32. Ezekiel 36:24
33. II Kings 17:19
34. Jeremiah 29:10
35. II Kings 17:13
36. Daniel 1:8
37. Daniel 6:10
38. Ezra 6:16
39. Esther 4:14
40. Nehemiah 1:9

SP 197-196

Maps

Abraham, Isaac, and Jacob

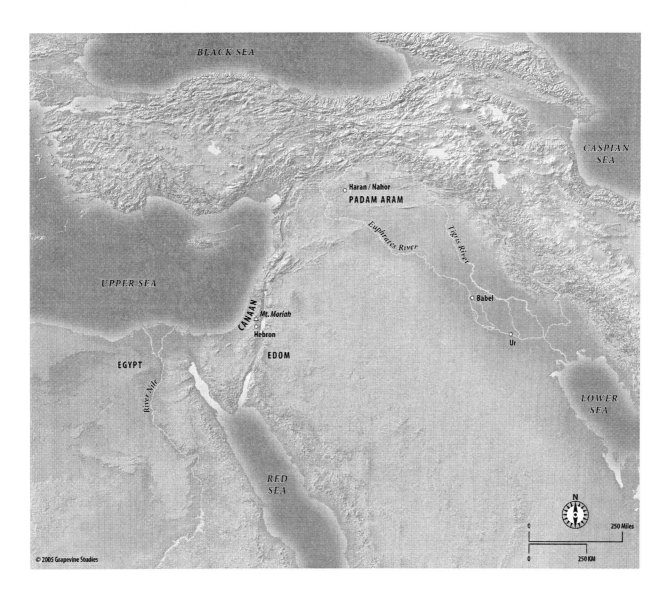

1. Label the Tigris River.

2. Label the Euphrates River.

3. Label the following cities:

- Babel

- Ur

- Haran

- Hebron

- Nahor

Joseph and Moses

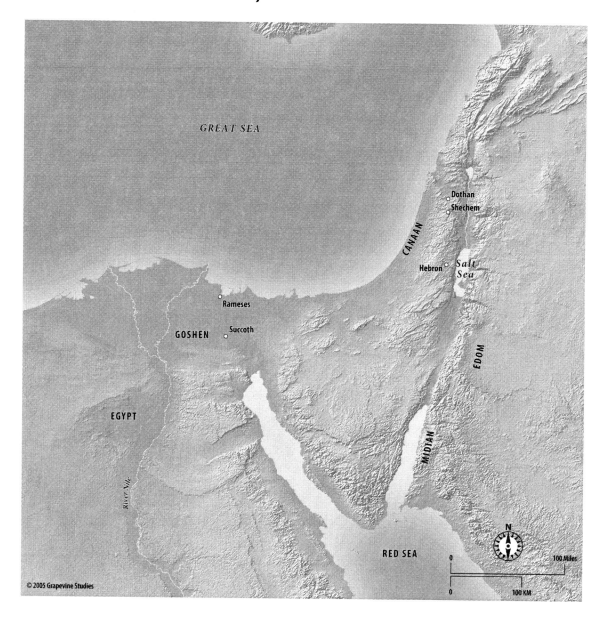

1. Label the River Nile
2. Label the country of Midian.
3. Label the Red Sea.
4. Label the following cities:
   - Hebron
   - Shechem
   - Dothan

   - Rameses
   - Succouth

The Promised Land

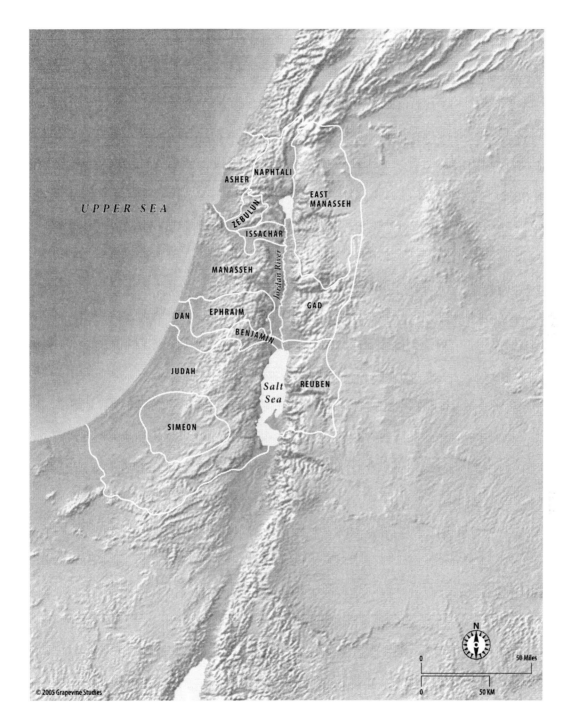

1. Label the Jordan River.
2. Label the Upper Sea.
3. Label the area allotted to each tribe.

Joshua to Samuel

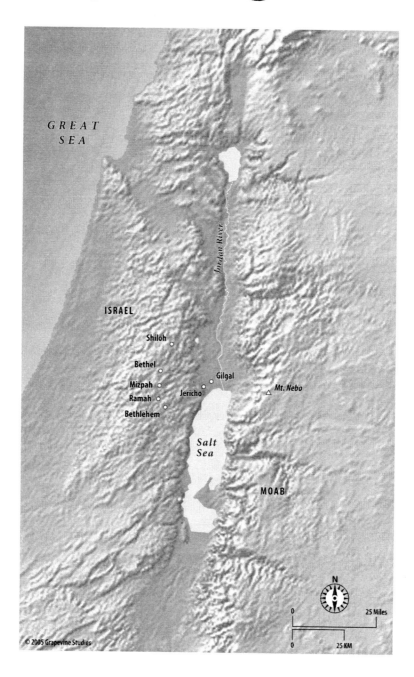

1. Label the countries of Moab and Israel.

2. Label the following cities:

- Gilgal
- Jericho
- Bethlehem
- Shiloh

- Bethel
- Mizpah
- Ramah

The Kings

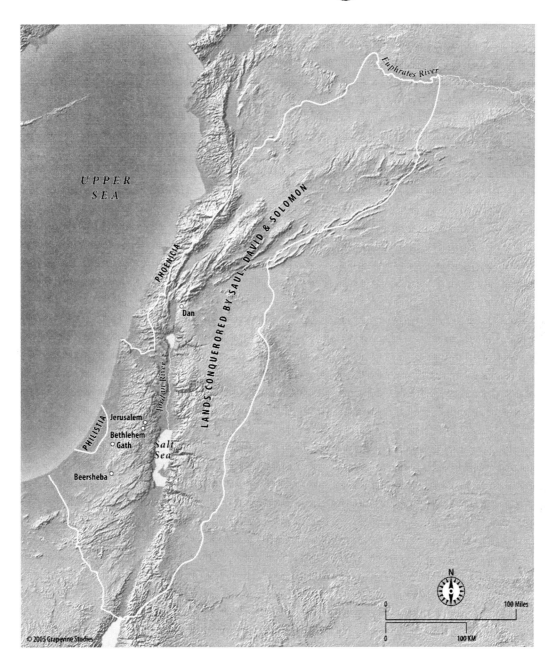

1. Label the country of Philistia and Phoencia
2. Label the land, "Lands conquered by Saul, David, and Solomon."
3. Label the following cities:

   - Bethlehem
   - Gath
   - Jerusalem

   - Beersheba
   - Dan

Assyria and Babylon

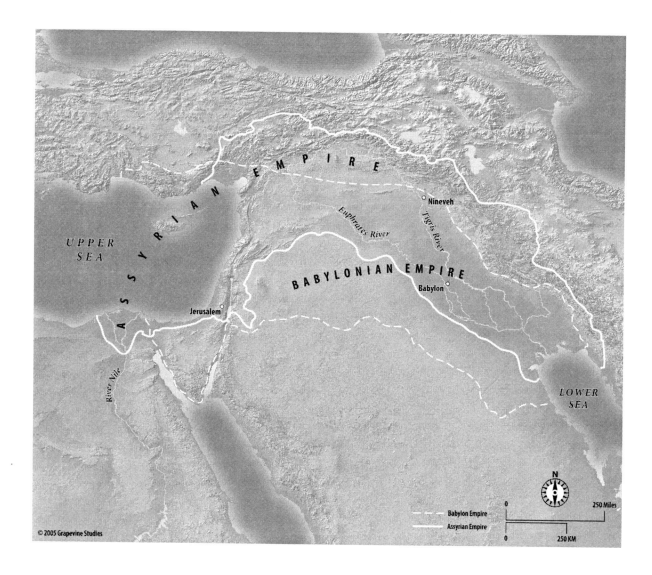

1. Label the Assyrian Empire and the Babylonian Empire.

2. Label the following cities:

   • Nineveh

   • Jerusalem

   • Babylon

Persia

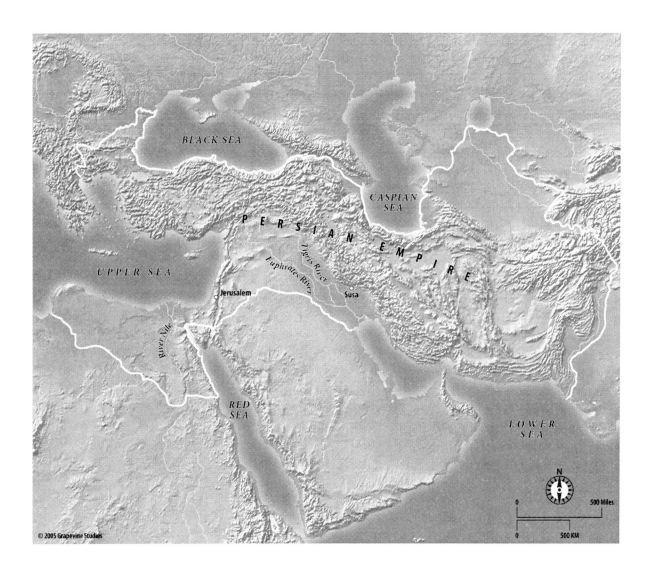

1. Label the Persian Empire.

2. Label the following cities:

   • Susa/Shushan

   • Jerusalem

Addendum

Once a Week Schedule

Week 1 & 2	Lesson 1	Week 28	Lesson 22
Week 3	Lesson 2	Week 29	Lesson 23
Week 4	Lesson 3	Week 30	Lesson 24
Week 5	Lesson 4	Week 31	Review 4
Week 6	Lesson 5	Week 32	Lesson 25
Week 7	Lesson 6	Week 33	Lesson 26
Week 8	Review 1	Week 34	Lesson 27
Week 9	Lesson 7	Week 35	Lesson 28
Week 10	Lesson 8	Week 36	Lesson 29
Week 11	Lesson 9	Week 37	Review 5
Week 12	Lesson 10	Week 38	Lesson 30
Week 13	Lesson 11	Week 39	Lesson 31
Week 14	Lesson 12	Week 40	Lesson 32
Week 15	Review 2	Week 41	Lesson 33
Week 16	Lesson 13	Week 42	Lesson 34
Week 17	Lesson 14	Week 43	Review 6
Week 18	Lesson 15	Week 44	Lesson 35
Week 19	Lesson 16	Week 45	Lesson 36
Week 20	Lesson 17	Week 46	Lesson 37
Week 21	Lesson 18	Week 47	Lesson 38
Week 22	Review 3	Week 48	Lesson 39
Week 23	Mid-Term Review	Week 49	Review 7
Week 24	Mid-Term Review	Week 50	Final Review
Week 25	Lesson 19	Week 51	Final Review
Week 26	Lesson 20	Week 52	FREE
Week 27	Lesson 21		

Daily Schedule

Day 1-4 (Level 3)	Lesson 1	Day 45	Cards and Quest
Day 1-3 (Level 4)	Lesson 1	Day 46	Lesson 12 Review page
		Day 47	Lesson 12 page 1
Day 4 (Level 4)	Lesson 2 Quest Page	Day 48	Lesson 12 page 2
Day 5	Lesson 2 page 1		
Day 6	Lesson 2 page 2	Day 49-50	Review 2
Day 7	Cards and Quest	Day 51	Cards and Quest
Day 8	Lesson 3 Review page	Day 52	Lesson 13 Review page
Day 9	Lesson 3 page 1	Day 53	Lesson 13 page 1
Day 10	Lesson 3 page 2	Day 54	Lesson 13 page 2
Day 11	Cards and Quest	Day 55	Cards and Quest
Day 12	Lesson 4 Review page	Day 56	Lesson 14 Review page
Day 13	Lesson 4 page 1	Day 57	Lesson 14 page 1
Day 14	Lesson 4 page 2	Day 58	Lesson 14 page 2
Day 15	Cards and Quest	Day 59	Cards and Quest
Day 16	Lesson 5 Review page	Day 60	Lesson 15 Review page
Day 17	Lesson 5 page 1	Day 61	Lesson 15 page 1
Day 18	Lesson 5 page 2	Day 62	Lesson 15 page 2
Day 19	Cards and Quest	Day 63	Cards and Quest
Day 20	Lesson 6 Review page	Day 64	Lesson 16 Review page
Day 21	Lesson 6 page 1	Day 65	Lesson 16 page 1
Day 22	Lesson 6 page 2	Day 66	Lesson 16 page 2
Day 23-24	Review 1	Day 67	Cards and Quest
Day 25	Cards and Quest	Day 68	Lesson 17 Review page
Day 26	Lesson 7 Review page	Day 69	Lesson 17 page 1
Day 27	Lesson 7 page 1	Day 70	Lesson 17 page 2
Day 28	Lesson 7 page 2	Day 71	Cards and Quest
Day 29	Cards and Quest		
		Day 72	Lesson 18 Review page
Day 30	Lesson 8 Review page	Day 73	Lesson 18 page 1
Day 31	Lesson 8 page 1	Day 74	Lesson 18 page 2
Day 32	Lesson 8 page 2		
Day 33	Cards and Quest	Day 75-76	Review 3
		Day 77-78	Mid-Term Review
Day 34	Lesson 9 Review page		
Day 35	Lesson 9 page 1	Day 79	Cards and Quest
Day 36	Lesson 9 page 2	Day 80	Lesson 19 Review page
Day 37	Cards and Quest	Day 81	Lesson 19 page 1
		Day 82	Lesson 19 page 2
Day 38	Lesson 10 Review page	Day 83	Cards and Quest
Day 39	Lesson 10 page 1		
Day 40	Lesson 10 page 2	Day 84	Lesson 20 Review page
Day 41	Cards and Quest	Day 85	Lesson 20 page 1
		Day 86	Lesson 20 page 2
Day 42	Lesson 11 Review page	Day 87	Cards and Quest
Day 43	Lesson 11 page 1		
Day 44	Lesson 11 page 2		

Day 88	Lesson 21 Review page		Day 131	Cards and Quest
Day 89	Lesson 21 page 1			
Day 90	Lesson 21 page 2		Day 132	Lesson 31 Review page
Day 91	Cards and Quest		Day 133	Lesson 31 page 1
			Day 134	Lesson 31 page 2
Day 92	Lesson 22 Review page		Day 135	Cards and Quest
Day 93	Lesson 22 page 1			
Day 94	Lesson 22 page 2		Day 136	Lesson 32 Review page
Day 95	Cards and Quest		Day 137	Lesson 32 page 1
			Day 138	Lesson 32 page 2
Day 96	Lesson 23 Review page		Day 139	Cards and Quest
Day 97	Lesson 23 page 1			
Day 98	Lesson 23 page 2		Day 140	Lesson 33 Review page
Day 99-100	Review 4		Day 141	Lesson 33 page 1
			Day 142	Lesson 33 page 2
Day 101	Cards and Quest		Day 143	Cards and Quest
Day 102	Lesson 24 Review page			
Day 103	Lesson 24 page 1		Day 144	Lesson 34 Review page
Day 104	Lesson 24 page 2		Day 145	Lesson 34 page 1
Day 105	Cards and Quest		Day 146	Lesson 34 page 2
Day 106	Lesson 25 Review page		Day 147-148	Review 6
Day 107	Lesson 25 page 1			
Day 108	Lesson 25 page 2		Day 149	Cards and Quest
Day 109	Cards and Quest		Day 150	Lesson 35 Review page
			Day 151	Lesson 35 page 1
Day 110	Lesson 26 Review page		Day 152	Lesson 35 page 2
Day 111	Lesson 26 page 1		Day 153	Cards and Quest
Day 112	Lesson 26page 2			
Day 113	Cards and Quest		Day 154	Lesson 36 Review page
			Day 155	Lesson 36 page 1
Day 114	Lesson 27 Review page		Day 156	Lesson 36 page 2
Day 115	Lesson 27 page 1		Day 157	Cards and Quest
Day 116	Lesson 27 page 2			
Day 117	Cards and Quest		Day 158	Lesson 37 Review page
			Day 159	Lesson 37 page 1
Day 118	Lesson 28 Review page		Day 160	Lesson 37 page 2
Day 119	Lesson 28 page 1		Day 161	Cards and Quest
Day 120	Lesson 28 page 2			
Day 121	Cards and Quest		Day 162	Lesson 38 Review page
			Day 163	Lesson 38 page 1
Day 122	Lesson 29 Review page		Day 164	Lesson 38 page 2
Day 123	Lesson 29 page 1		Day 165	Cards and Quest
Day 124	Lesson 29 page 2			
			Day 166	Lesson 39 Review page
Day 125-126	Review 5		Day 167	Lesson 39 page 1
			Day 168	Lesson 39 page 2
Day 127	Cards and Quest			
Day 128	Lesson 30 Review page		Day 169-170	Review 7
Day 129	Lesson 30 page 1			
Day 130	Lesson 30 page 2		Day 171-175	Final Review

Congratulations on your completion of the Old Testament Overview!

Continue your journey through the Bible with the Level 3 New Testament Overview! Students will learn:

- The New Testament Timeline
- Basic New Testament Geography
- See how Jesus restores the broken relationship between God and man.
- Learn about the people, events, and places of the New Testament.

Continue your journey through the Bible with the Level 4 New Testament Overview! Students will learn:

- The New Testament Timeline
- Learn where the New Testament books fit in chronologically, who wrote the books, and to whom were they written.
- See how Jesus restores the broken relationship between God and man.
- Continue to master the use of Bible study tools.

Order your
New Testament Overview Course
Today!

By Phone

877-436-2317

On Line

www.grapevinestudies.com

303

Recommended Resources from
Grapevine Studies

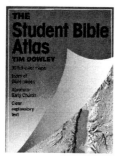

Student Bible Atlas

This colorful atlas includes 30 maps that will give your students a clear understanding of where biblical events took place. Your student will be able to trace the journeys of Abraham, cross the Red Sea with Moses and follow the missionary journeys of Paul.

Atlas of the Holy Lands

Older students will enjoy this wonderfully which includes 80 maps, helpful illustrations, information thematic maps and much more! will be able to use this atlas to make their Bible life.

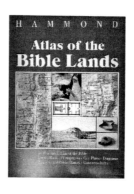

illustrated atlas archaeological Your student study come to

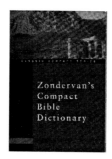

Every student needs basic Bible study resources: a Concordance, Bible Dictionary, and Topical Bible. Your student will find these concise and conveniently sized resources perfect for their first references! Teachers can also use this 3 book set for gifts or prizes!

Order Today!

By Phone

877-436-2317

On Line

www.grapevinestudies.com

Grapevine Studies Curriculums

Old and New Testament Overview Books

Beginner (Ages 5-7)

Beginner students will enjoy this hands-on study of the major characters and events of the Bible using simple, colorful stick figures, and symbols. Teachers will appreciate the chronological and easy-to-teach format! At the end of the year your students will have learned 40+ memory verses and will have created their first Bible study resource book! One-year study.

Level 1 (Grades 1-2)

Level 1 students will begin to learn the Old or New Testament Timeline, with each subsequent lesson related to a point on the timeline. Teachers will see measurable results in just a few lessons! In one year your students should be able to recite 38+ memory verses, fill out the timeline and tell you several facts about each character or event on the timeline. One-year study.

Level 2 (Grades 3-4)

Level 2 students will expand their knowledge of the Bible timeline while learning new facts about each timeline character and event. Memory work includes the books of the Bible in order and by category. One-year study.

    Old Testament memory work: Ten Commandments and the Twelve Sons of Jacob.

    New Testament Memory work: Twelve Apostles and the Apostle's Creed.

Level 3 (Grades 5-8)

Level 3 students will deepen their understanding of the Old or New Testament characters and events. Students should be able to complete either the Old or New Testament Timeline on their own. In addition, students will be introduced to basic biblical geography, so they will not only know what happened but where it happened! One-year study.

Level 4 (Teen-Adult)

Level 4 students will master the Old or New Testament Timeline and know where the books of the Bible fit into the chronology of the Timeline. Students will also be introduced to and practice using basic Bible study tools: a Bible Concordance, A Bible Dictionary, and a Topical Bible with each lesson. Students will also be challenged with critical thinking questions associated with each lesson. One-year study.

Level 5 (Teen-Adult)

Take a self-directed approach to studying the Old or New Testament. Students will take notes, use Bible study resources, and answer critical thinking questions in each lesson. Hands-on activities and research projects make this an excellent study for students who desire to move to deepen their understanding of the Bible. Start your study today! No teacher manuals needed. One-year study.

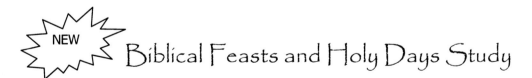

NEW Biblical Feasts and Holy Days Study

Learn what God expected from His people when they celebrated and observed the feasts and holy days. Discover how Jesus has fulfilled the spring feasts with His first appearance. Read about what New Testament events that occurred on or around the feasts and holy days. This study will give you a better understanding of the New Testament and all that Jesus did for us. Begin your 13 week study today! *Available in both the Stick Figure curriculum and Blueprint curriculum.*

Congratulations on your completion of the Old Testament Overview! We, at Grapevine Studies, pray that this study has been a blessing to you and your students! We would love to hear from you!!

Send your comments to:

Email

info@grapevinestudies.com

Snail mail

PO Box 2123
Glenrock, WY 82637-2123

Order your
New Testament Overview Course
Today!

Website

www.grapevinestudies.com